a month
of sundays

JAMES O'LOGHLIN

a month of sundays

how to go travelling without leaving town

ALLEN&UNWIN

First published in 2004

83 Alexander Street,
Crows Nest NSW 2065 Australia
Phone: (61 2) 8425 0100
Fax: (61 2) 9906 2218
E-mail: info@allenandunwin.com
Web: www.allenandunwin.com

National Library of Australia
Cataloguing-in-Publication entry:

O'Loghlin, James.
  A Month of Sundays: how to go travelling without leaving town.

  ISBN 1 74114 367 5.

  1. Sydney (N.S.W.) - Guidebooks. 2. Sydney (N.S.W.) -
  Description and travel. I. Title

  919.44104

Set in 11/14 pt Minion by Midland Typesetters, Maryborough, Victoria
Printed in Australia by McPherson's Printing Group

10 9 8 7 6 5 4 3 2 1

In memory of my mother, Gillian,
and to my father Graham.
And to my companions, Lucy and Bibi.

contents

one

the invasion

At 7 a.m. on Monday 1 September 2003, the day Lucy and I celebrated our eighth not-married-but-together anniversary, we were fast asleep in bed with our ten-month-old daughter Bibi lying chaperone between us when the crash of breaking glass startled us awake. Bibi wailed. I jumped out of bed and crept to our window. Three men were attacking the front of the house next door with sledgehammers and crowbars. They were crashing in windows and bashing through walls.

I sighed. It had begun.

As Lucy tried to comfort Bibi, I lay staring at the ceiling, listening to the racket and getting more depressed. The builders had arrived. It wasn't a surprise. We'd known they were coming, we just hadn't known when.

Ten months earlier the house under assault, number eighteen, had sold for the third time in the two and a half years since we had moved into number twenty. It was a roomy, sunny three-bedroom house in good nick, but none of the people who had

1

bought it in that time wanted to live in it until they had knocked it down and built something much, much bigger.

It was a trend.

More and more homes in North Bondi were beginning to look as if they were on steroids, with bits jutting up and out every possible which-way to fit as much house as possible onto the available land. Everyone thought themselves an expert on property and renovating and it was hard to have a neighbourhood conversation without the subject popping up. Everyone who moved in thought a house wasn't really a house unless you had pulled it apart and put it back together again so that it had polished floorboards, aluminium-framed windows and more bedrooms than there were people living there. The big rich houses also had to have a pool, a home theatre and something called a void, a room-sized piece of nothing that proved you were so rich you could afford to waste space.

This had led to the demise of the front garden. No one ever, ever had any trouble parking outside their home in North Bondi. It's just far enough away from the beach to put it out of reach of visitors. Yet all over the place people were ripping up their gardens and putting in carports. They obviously thought that the security they got from having their car that extra two metres closer to the house at night and the importance of protecting its roof from rain far outweighed any pleasure you could get from plants, trees and grass.

This meant there were two types of people in our street—those who had a front garden full of car and those who had a front garden full of front garden. The former usually had a front fence that wasn't actually a fence at all, but was a concrete wall a metre and a half high, while the latter preferred a real fence of the old-style low-slung picket variety.

Those with carports and walls would rarely be seen except through the window of their four-wheel-drive as it pulled in and out of their ex-front garden, whereas those with front gardens spent time in them and so met and talked to each other. We had a little front garden, and whenever I felt like a chat I'd go and sit on the front steps. Sooner or later one of the neighbours who also had a front garden would appear and we'd talk. No pressure, no commitment, just a friendly little chat about nothing in particular that either of us could pull the pin on as soon as we wanted.

Sometimes I would see carport/garage/concrete wall-people squeezing past their car and then sort of milling around outside their wall and I'd wonder what they were doing. After a while I realised that they wanted to get in on the neighbourhood chat too, but it was harder for them because they'd buggered their house up by accidentally turning it into a fortress.

The problem for each of the successive buyers of number eighteen was the vertical backyard. It was about 15 metres long and rose steeply from floor level at the rear of the house until, at the back of the block, it was at the same height as the top of the roof. Our house, a semi, had a similarly vertically challenged backyard. We had dug some of it out so that we now had what a real estate agent would describe as a 'Three Level Multi Function Leisure Area' and what anyone else would call a hill with three ledges cut into it.

Each time number eighteen had sold, the same thing had happened. A few weeks after the sale the new owner would appear in the vertical backyard with an experty-type person holding a folder. The new owner would outline his dream, pointing and drawing pictures in the air. We'd hear him say words like 'pool', 'level', 'landscaped' and 'dream home'. Each time the experty person would look down at their folder, shake their head and utter words like 'cliff', 'joking', 'excavation' and 'millions'. The hill would smile smugly to itself and soon after the For Sale sign would go up again.

Ivan, the latest owner, was different. It wasn't the fact that he got rid of the tenants as soon as their lease was up that showed us he meant business, and it wasn't the fact that we got his proposed plans from council in the mail so soon after he'd bought the place. It wasn't even that he started to excavate the vertical backyard. What convinced us that Ivan meant business was *how* he excavated the vertical backyard. He didn't use a bobcat, a labourer or a shovel. He did it himself and used a milk crate. It was midsummer, temperatures were in the high thirties, he was a thin, pale, bearded man over fifty and he spent days dragging dirt from the top of the backyard to the bottom, using as his sole tool a milk crate. It didn't work very well. A milk crate is, in fact, a pretty crap tool for large-scale soil excavation. Most of the dirt just fell through the holes—but he kept going.

'How's it going, Ivan?' I'd say whenever I saw him over the back fence.

He'd never reply. He wasn't being rude, it was just that he was panting so hard he was physically unable to speak. He would just wave weakly, with an expression on his face that suggested death would be a relief.

I'd then offer to call an ambulance, and he'd shake his head and sadly return to the hill in the same way that a torture victim might return to the rack after being given a five-minute breather. Ivan meant business. Even the hill started to look nervous.

Ivan's plans weren't good. Actually, that's not fair. If you wanted to buy a normal house, knock it down and build a mansion, they were good. Perfect, in fact. But they weren't good for us. They showed a huge, two-storey, five-bedroom plus void house with a garage and big concrete wall 140 centimetres from our house.

The house would block out most of our sun and substitute the pleasant view of rooftops we enjoyed from the top of our vertical backyard for one of just his roof. But what worried me most was the thought of living next to a building site.

The three of us spent a lot of time at home. Some people say that having a baby prevents them going out, but one of the many things Bibi had given us was an excuse. We didn't go out a lot before she arrived, and once she arrived we didn't have to give reasons. I took a sort of pride in the fact that I shut down on weekends, lazed about, read books and watched the footy with the sound down and classical music playing. I'd regularly have weekends where I left the house only twice—on Saturday to play touch footy (badly, but with enthusiasm) and on Sunday to go for a walk along the beach (quite well, but it's not a very hard thing to do). My idea of the perfect weekend was most other people's idea of the most boring weekend in the world.

I liked being at home. There were no hassles at home. I felt in control. I understood how home worked, I lived in it and, in combination with Lucy and the bank, I owned it. At home I didn't need to be alert, I rarely got alarmed and I could do what I wanted when I wanted. I could forget about trying to be entertaining and interesting and just be me.

When I was old enough for my parents to start leaving me home alone I used to feel an incredible sense of relief as their car drove off. Not because I didn't like them—I did—but because I was alone and free. King of the castle. The desire to lock the world out for a day or two a week remained strong.

Lucy wasn't like that. She liked to get out and do things, and usually did. But I'd often find excuses to duck her suggestions that on weekends we drive to Palm Beach or Cronulla or even nearby Bronte because, quite frankly, I couldn't be bothered.

Central to the idea of home as a place to lock out, and find relief from, the world was that by shutting the door you could effectively say goodbye to it. But construction work happening six days a week for goodness knows how long—similar jobs in the area (and there were plenty of them) seemed to drag on forever—threatened that whole idea.

It wouldn't have been so bad if I'd worked normal hours. Usually if there's a builder next door, they work when you work, but my job was hosting an evening radio show on the ABC, which meant I had my leisure time at the start of the day.

This suited me. There was plenty of time to hang out with Bibi, and because there's nothing good on television at that time of the day there was no risk of spending my free hours staring at the box. People would express sympathy for me because of my hours, saying that it must be terrible not to be free at nights. I'd nod solemnly, and keep to myself the joys of sleeping in and lazing around in the morning.

I wouldn't call it challenging, but it was certainly pleasant. We'd often talk about making more use of the time, but never really did. Sleeping in, brekky, playing with Bibi, then off to work became the routine.

But when you have the sound of Johnno screaming at Bazza to 'Grab some more of the fucking four inches!' mixed in with some electrical drilly thing, set against the background of loud, loud, loud mobile phone ads broken up by non-stop blocks of whatever it is they play now on Triple M (provided by the radio in the truck parked right outside the front of our bedroom) it's very hard to feel like you're king of the castle. You feel like the castle is being invaded.

By 9 a.m. the dust from the demolition was drifting through our windows and Bibi was rubbing her eyes. We decided there was only one thing to do. Run away. Or at least walk. We went down to the beach and had breakfast in a café. We talked about renting, we talked about selling, we talked about house-minding, we talked about buying a giant mansion-sized soundproof box and asking them to work inside it.

'We could sleep in the car,' I said. 'We could drive to a park and sleep there under the stars and if it rains get in the car and then at least we won't get woken up at seven by jackhammers. I mean, I never get to sleep before one because you just can't come home from work and go straight to sleep and I'm going to get overtired and grumpy and fall asleep at the wheel and have a car crash and . . .'

'Calm down,' said Lucy.

She was right. I was losing it. But it felt good.

'What if we bought something even louder than the drills and the smashing and the Triple M combined, something like . . . a Concorde, but a stationary one, and we turned that on? Maybe then they'd hate it so much they'd leave.'

This time she just looked at me. So did Bibi.

'We can either move out or we can stay,' Lucy said. Totally ridiculous. Or was it? I looked at her through narrowed eyes. She seemed remarkably together, but then again I was only comparing her to me.

'We can't stay. How can we stay?' I said quickly. Too quickly, but I couldn't help it.

'We could stay,' she said extra calmly, which was good. If she'd let the panic I was feeling get to her too, we'd have been doomed. One of us had to stay calm, and I was glad it was her. It meant I could go on running down the road to hysteria.

'How can we stay? We can't stay, because if we stay it'll all be bad and worse and everything and . . .'

'We could stay,' she repeated firmly and slowly, 'and we could go as well.'

'Huh?'

'We don't need to be in the house when they're there.'

'But it'll be from dawn to dusk five days a week. Six! They'll work Saturdays.'

'We can go and do things. In the morning. All the things we don't usually do.'

I was suspicious. 'What "things"?'

'Go to the park. Go to the zoo. The aquarium. Explore Sydney. I've lived here for 34 years, you for . . . how many?'

'Eighteen. I moved here in 1985.'

'And Bibi one. Between us, that's, um . . .'

'Fifty-three years.'

'Exactly. Think of all the things we haven't done or seen. We could go to Lakemba.'

'What's at Lakemba?'

'Exactly. We won't know unless we go.'

'Um . . .' I was playing for time. This felt like a threat to the way I did things. 'Aren't your parents going away to Turkey? Maybe we could go and stay at their place.' It was just up the road at Bondi Junction.

'We could, but they're not going until October.'

'So we've got a month till then.'

'A month. A month to do things and see things, the things that most people can only do on weekends,' said Lucy. 'We've got a month of Sundays.'

I suppose it was one way of looking at it.

two

a bad place to busk

Our plan was to do all those things that you were supposed to do on Sundays, but which we never got around to doing. The sort of things we used to do on Sundays when we were kids. Both Lucy and I had memories of Sundays being about packing the car and going somewhere new. For me in Canberra, it was often into the bush for a walk, or a picnic near a river. I would always take a book to read on the way there, but never quite get around to opening it because I wanted to see what was around the next corner. Then there was the anticipation of arriving and exploring, poking about down the river or seeing where a bush track led. My favourite places were those where there was no one else in sight, and I would imagine we were discovering the place for the first time. That, in the old days, was a Sunday.

That sense of discovery was what we wanted to recapture, but how could we in a city we had both lived in for so long? The answer was to start thinking like tourists. Whenever I visited somewhere new, whether it was Paris or Parkes, I'd spend a couple of hours wandering about trying to get a feel for the place. But I never did that in Sydney. Everywhere I went was for a purpose. I'd go, do what I had to do, then come home. If I went to a friend's house in a part of town I'd never been to before, I'd go straight there and come straight back. The more I thought about it, the more I realised that there were all sorts of places within a hour's drive of home that I had no idea about.

Sitting on the train on the way to work that day, I realised that the pattern of my life had become entirely predictable. I woke up, I hung out, I went to work, I came home and I went to sleep again. Sometimes I'd go to the movies or to one of six parks or three beaches, or to visit one or two of a couple of dozen friends.

My life wasn't boring. I liked most of it and it was all pretty comfortable, but I clung to my patterns. Pretty much all my life occurred at home or at work, or at a few other places within 10 kilometres of where I lived. If anyone ever wanted to assassinate me it'd be easy. They'd know exactly where I was going to be pretty much any time, any day.

And the day after I got assassinated, when I was having my exit interview and it was put to me that for years and years I had spent week after week after week doing pretty much exactly the same thing and following pretty much exactly the same not-all-that-challenging routine, how would I feel?

Slightly embarrassed, I think.

So this was my chance to break those patterns, to go places I had never been before and explore them, like Marco Polo and Vasco da Gama and Captain Cook had before me. Well, not quite like them, because they went places that *no one* had ever been before, whereas we were just going to go to places that *we* hadn't been before and, okay, maybe exploring different areas of the city in which we'd lived for many years wasn't quite as exciting as travelling halfway around the world and discovering new continents and civilisations and bringing back gunpowder and beef and black bean sauce and whatever else Marco Polo brought back, but the point was that we would be exploring—seeing new things, breaking patterns and, most importantly, getting away from those loud bastards with their drills and their radios.

And the other important point was that in accepting this idea I had stopped panicking about the builders and the impact they were going to have on my life and now had at least an illusion of control. That was very important.

That night we made a list of places to go. We agreed that we should ease into it. Or at least I insisted. Whereas we planned to normally only go to places neither of us had been to before or knew much about, our first destination was familiar. Bronte Park.

The next morning the demolition continued so we had no trouble motivating ourselves to get going. I don't have a lot of sympathy for property developers, but there must be an anxious period when the first thing you do after buying a very expensive asset is destroy it. After just one day the nice family home Ivan had bought looked like something out of a war zone. In real estate talk, 'A Little Bit of Beirut in the East.'

Bronte Park is at Bronte Beach. Unlike most beachside parks, which are merely strips of grass that separate road and sand, it's a huge green expanse that eventually thins into a tree-lined gorge and runs deep back into the suburb. At the south end of the park—and the beach—are what used to be the Bronte shops and are now the Bronte cafés. Ten years ago there was the normal variety of suburban shops, newsagent, greengrocer, mini-mart, etc. One by one they all became cafés. There are eight in a row, with a fish and chippery at the end thrown in for variety. It's an indication that Bronte—like all Sydney's eastern suburbs beaches—is now primarily for visitors.

I couldn't help feeling for the locals. The only way to buy milk at the Bronte shops now is to order a cold flat white without the coffee, and if you need some bread you have to either order a goat's cheese, asparagus and prosciutto focaccia without the goat's cheese, asparagus and prosciutto, or nick half a slice of sourdough from someone who hasn't quite finished their scrambled eggs with the lot.

What makes Bronte so beautiful is the way the park and beach connect. At Bondi there is a beautiful park and a beautiful beach, which are for some reason separated by an ugly carpark. To get from the grass and the playground to the sand you have to look to your left, look to your right, then look to your left again. Not having to do that ups the relaxation factor considerably. There is plenty of parking at Bronte but it's tucked out of the way.

While the visitor population is high on weekends, locals do exist and this morning one particular variety was in abundance—the sixty-something newly retired ocker male. There were a couple of dozen of them spread around, none wearing anything other than Speedos, and all with those impossible beer guts that are attached to otherwise fit-looking bodies and seeming as if they have no right to be there. They appear affixed in the same way as a grass catcher is to a lawnmower, and it would be no surprise to see someone whip his off and empty the contents (presumably 15 litres of VB) into the bin.

They lie in groups in the sun and all talk a bit louder than necessary, as people who reckon they own the joint do. Even though we had just emerged from winter, they were already ridiculously brown, with skin the colour and texture of desert boots.

One was talking to a similarly aged German woman whose English wasn't all that good.

'WE CALL THEM THONGS,' he shouted, pointing to his footwear. 'NOT FLIP-FLOPS. NO NOEY. YES. THONGS. GOOD FOR THE SHOWER. YES?'

The woman looked nervous. I wondered if I should go over and explain that his shouting wasn't meant to be aggressive, just slightly patronising. But she probably wouldn't understand me either, and I'd end up shouting too. Then she'd be doubly nervous.

'THANK YOU FOR SUCH KIND OFFER,' she replied, just as loudly, 'BUT I HAVE SHOWER AT HOME. I WILL HAVE SHOWER ALONE. NOT WITH YOU. THANK YOU.'

'NO. I DIDN'T MEAN . . . AHHH!' and with that frustrated sound he threw his arms up, turned on his heel and strode off with a peculiar legs-tied-together-with-an-invisible-rope-so-can-only-take-very-small-steps gait.

We picked a spot in the grass under a tree on a bank, just high enough that we could see the sea. Bibi explored the vicinity. A guy played guitar under another tree. At first it seemed idyllic, but then I noticed he kept looking around and I worried he might be the world's worst-located busker. There's not much passing traffic in a big fat park on a Tuesday morning.

Up the north end of the park near the swings and play-grounds were the mums and bubs. They hunt in packs, the mums, up to fifteen clustered tight in picnic circles, with three-wheeled racing prams strategically placed covered-wagon-style around the outside in case of attack. Around lunchtime a couple of dads arrived from the office, one going so far as to remove his tie for 23 minutes of quality time before the free enterprise system claimed him back.

Bibi and I escorted Lucy to the seawater pool, which looked inviting but felt freezing. After dipping her toe in, then pulling it out very quickly, Lucy would have changed her mind—but luckily, when in the car she had recklessly declared she was going to go for a swim, I had had the foresight to cement her bold declaration into a 50-cent bet. She was trapped.

In the time it took her to descend three steps to be waist deep, a local had stripped off, got in and swum five laps at the sort of pace that would have had him being overtaken by a floating twig. When Lucy was rib deep he was onto lap eight.

'Look, Beeb, there's Mummy shivering.'

'Shut up.'

'It's easier if you just jump straight in, you know.'

'It might also be easier if you jammed one of my sandals into your mouth.'

'Hey, it's only 50 cents.'

But she hadn't heard. As if I had become Laurie Lawrence, my words had motivated action beyond normal human capabilities. She had dived in. I looked at the old local, now halfway down lap nine. He had a big start, but Luce was fired up. She'd catch him in minutes. She'd zoom up and down and . . .

'Okay. Pay up.'

Lucy was beside me, shaking and covered in towel. She had virtually teleported onto the edge of the pool, so fast had she got out.

When she stopped shaking, we wandered back up the park past the little train that ran round a 100-metre track in the park. It was packed away this day in a little train-shaped house. We sat down and I lay back and thought how brilliantly clever I had been to escape the builders. All right, how brilliantly clever we had been. Okay, Lucy had been. But I'd agreed.

I thought about the importance of peace and quiet for mental health, how necessary it was to . . . Wwwwaaaaaaaaaaaa!!!!

What the hell was that?

14

An engine.

A really loud engine.

So loud you had to shout your thoughts to hear them inside your head.

What, had they followed us here? Was the demolishing of number eighteen merely a cover to hide their real aim of driving us mad? I looked up. No planes. Then around. No tractors, no cars, no lawnmowers. There! A leafblower. A guy from the council with a leafblower. A really loud leafblower. And he knew it was loud too. That's why he had earmuffs on.

The train of thoughts flowing through my mind was instantly replaced by the repeating loop of *This leafblower is really loud, I hope it stops soon, I wonder if, after he does this path, he's going to do that other path. This leafblower is really loud, I hope it stops soon, I wonder if, after he does this path, he's going to do that other path. This leafblower is . . .*

The quiet was gone. The peace was gone. I wondered why no one had been able to invent something that did what a leafblower did but was quiet. Then I realised they had. It's called a broom and it's not only quieter but cheaper, easier to carry and environmentally friendlier. And brooms don't break down. But they do take just a little bit of effort to operate and that, obviously, disqualifies them as suitable council equipment.

'Owwwhhhh,' I said.

Lucy was strangely unperplexed.

'Don't worry, he's just cleaning the paths.'

'But it's so loud.' I got out my phone. 'I'm going to ring the council and complain.'

'Don't ring the council.'

'The council are supposed to be making our lives better, not worse. If he had a broom, he could do exactly the same thing, except it'd be quiet and he'd be getting some exercise which would be good for him. I'm ringing them.'

I started dialling.

'They'll think you're a nut.'

I stopped dialling. She was right. I didn't want to be that crazy guy who hates leafblowers. Leafblowers are probably part of world's best practice. Perhaps there's an occupational health and safety regulation prohibiting brooms as being needlessly wearing to backs and shoulders.

I sighed.

'Do you reckon this is some sort of conspiracy?' I said.

three
two jewels in legoland

That night when I got home, number eighteen was nearly completely gone. It had deteriorated from a little bit of Beirut in the east to a ruin you could use as a setting for the battle scenes in *Saving Private Ryan 2: Return to France*. It must be the fun part, demolishing. I'd paid 50 cents once at a school fete for 60 seconds in which I could do whatever I wanted to an old car with a sledgehammer. Even though all the good bits such as the windscreen, dashboard and engine had already been thoroughly smashed in and all I managed was to bash fairly unspectacularly at a door, denting it slightly, it was still fun. And next door they were getting paid for it. I should have volunteered.

I wondered if demolishers ever got the wrong address.

'Oh, that's a *five*. Yes, I see now. Sorry, it sort of looked like a seven, see. Um, we'll get that front wall of your house back up as soon as we can. Although we've got a bit on at the moment.'

On day two at 9 a.m. we arrived at Darling Harbour. Darling Harbour is a mass of walkways, harbour strolls, parks, restaurants, bars, playgrounds, movie theatres and spaces built around a harbour. It was created as a leisure, culture and business area in the 1980s by the New South Wales state government on the site of the old Sydney wharves. Everything is bright, colourful, shiny and new. All the bits fit together properly and everything works. You can walk in the sun near the water, there's a playground for the kids, a park to have lunch in and lots of quick places to have a bite or a drink. It's got everything except character.

Darling Harbour looks as if it has been assembled from an Ikea kit. It's what would happen if Starbucks went into harbour-side recreation areas. It has all the individuality and local character of a McDonald's and you can't help but suspect that there are hundreds of identical Darling Harbours spread around the world.

The fact that it just sprang up from a demolition site means that it is primarily a place of commerce, not life. No one lives there. No one has been going there for years. There are no regulars, except a few who drift down from the city during corporate lunchtime. In its many cafés, restaurants and shops you can be assured of efficient service, but don't expect to get chatting to any of the staff. They're there to do a job. So is Darling Harbour.

So we weren't going to visit Darling Harbour. We were going to walk through it to reach the two jewels that lie within.

The first is the Chinese Gardens. I had walked past the gardens a hundred times and never thought of going in. On Wednesday 3 September, we went in.

'Why pay four bucks to walk through a garden, Chinese or otherwise?' I commented.

'We'll see when we get in,' replied Lucy.

'Gardens are everywhere. There's one outside our back door. And if that's not big enough, what about the Botanic Gardens? They're free. And they've got a harbour view.'

'I don't think you're entering into the spirit of this properly.'

So we went. We paid our money and stepped inside and within minutes I realised four bucks was a bargain.

Officially it is the Chinese Garden of Friendship, brought to us by Sydney's Chinese sister city, Guangzhou. Paths wind around a lake, through trees to elegant Chinese pavilions, places perfect for sitting and not thinking about anything at all. Waterfalls cascade over rocks into lagoons. Somehow each pond, each bridge, each willow tree, each lotus plant is in exactly the right spot. None dominate, all combine to create tranquillity. It is like being in a float tank with a view.

We sat and watched the lake for a while, then explored the many paths that led around corners and past rocks to hidden pavilions or nooks. The gardens slope upwards at the back and paths wind their way through clumps of trees to emerge at the top next to a waterfall overlooking the lake.

At the top of the garden I was reminded by an incongruous glimpse of skyscraper between trees that we were in the middle of a city, but its hustle and bustle seemed a million miles away.

The gardens are so well set out that even with lots of visitors, there's plenty of room to find your own little sitting space. There's a display of bonsai trees, which made even Bibi feel tall. Or would have if the peace of the place hadn't persuaded her to sleep within a few minutes. Lucy and I had been having an argument as we arrived but we forgot what it was about. I still can't remember. All I know is that I was right.

Some of the visitors were obviously tourists, but others looked as though they had come in just to sit and read a book for a bit. Or just sit. I know someone who worked in the money market, doing a highly paid job I don't understand, who said he had to factor in a one-hour massage each day as part of his work routine to cope with stress. The Chinese Gardens would have been cheaper and just as effective.

The whole picture created a sense of safety and harmony. Doctors and bosses who detect signs of insecurity or paranoia in patients or staff should write out a prescription for the Chinese Gardens. If you're sick of being alert and alarmed, go.

You can even dress up in traditional Chinese dress for a photo. I know that sounds tacky, but the nine-year-olds love it and somehow it doesn't look tacky, just sweet. I don't know if Sydney has returned the favour to Guangzhou and designed an 'Aussie Gardens' there, but if we have I'd love to see the Chinese nine-year-olds dressed in stubbies, tank tops and cork hats.

The paths eventually converge on the Chinese teahouse. It's a welcome contrast to other Darling Harbour eating spots. It doesn't gleam but it's clean, it fits into its environment and those who work there don't look like unemployed models or have attitude to match. And the pork buns are good.

We emerged as you might from the surf, refreshed and ready for whatever was next, which happened to be the other jewel within Darling Harbour, Sydney Aquarium. Entertainment fun-complex thingys such as aquariums, fun parks, and places that have 'world' as the last part of their name ('Dream . . . ', 'Sea . . . ', 'Movie . . .') are always a gamble. They cost a CD to get into and you can't tell before you pay whether they are going to contain a day's worth of pleasure or just a lot of long queues for things that aren't really worth the wait. Unlike in shops, you don't get to see the goods before you buy. And we're hood-winked by memory into thinking they're fantastic. I remember from childhood the thrilling big dipper, the amazing wildcat ride and the rush of fun and fear as the fabulous river jet tipped over the edge and flew me down a near-vertical waterfall. But I've forgotten how long I had to wait to get a go on them, and whether I left Luna Park, the Easter Show or Sea World thinking that I'd had a fantastic time or that there had been seven seconds of thrilling fun interrupting a day that was otherwise hot, crowded and boring.

Like the Chinese Gardens, the aquarium doesn't impress from the outside. There's no smiling giant octopus beckoning you in. It's a plain white rectangular warehouse that looks as if it might be full of shipping containers.

But inside, you forget about Darling Harbour and builders and bills and what was on the telly last night, because of the open-mouthed fascination the fish provoke. It's better than art. Like the gardens, the aquarium removes, or at least hides, life's cares. The gardens do it by provoking relaxation. The aquarium uses awe.

For example, the seal tank. It's huge. You can look from above and see the seals splashing and flopping, or sunning themselves on a rock and shoving their tummies at the sun. Those sunning themselves look like the locals at Bronte, lazing and stretching about as if they own the place. They even have the beer guts.

Down below we strolled along a glass-covered walkway 2 metres below water level that led right through the middle of the tank, and saw seals swimming next to and above us. Their awkwardness on land was replaced underwater by a zooming, swooping grace. They did somersaults and leapt into the air, and looked to be having the best time in the world.

I wondered, though, if they were just making the best of it. The only difference between aquariums (and zoos) and jails is that animals are supposed to be so dumb they either don't mind or don't notice living in a cage. The aquarium is such a feel-good place and creates so much enjoyment for us humans that I desperately hoped we hadn't underestimated how smart the animals were and how pissed off it might be making them.

There's no noticeable sign of misery, though, unless leaping out of the water and doing underwater somersaults are a seal's cry for help. They don't look bored or stir crazy. Watching them swimming and sunning themselves made me wonder which species really had it all worked out. Obviously we're smarter and more advanced—seals haven't even invented the telephone. So why do we spend so much time wishing we were doing what they do? Where did we go wrong? One day, one of us got sick of carrying heavy stuff around and invented the wheel and the next thing you know we've got traffic jams and road rage.

But perhaps we'd get bored if we spent each day sitting on a rock and jumping in the ocean whenever we got too hot. The old blokes at Bronte didn't look bored, though.

The seals reminded me of Shelagh's cat. Shelagh was Mrs Haines, my fifth form English teacher, who, one hot afternoon as we trudged through Shakespeare, told the class about her cat. The cat, she said, sat on the windowsill in the sun all day, rarely upset, purring happily. Would any of us, she asked, like to swap places with her.

Sampson's hand shot up. 'I would,' he said.

'Why, Anthony?'

'I've always wanted to know what it was like to be female.'

Sampson often missed the point but he usually got a laugh.

What she was trying to get us to think about was whether we'd prefer more contentment if it meant less self-awareness. Of course, we were meant to come down on the side of self-awareness and the challenges of being human, but when you see the water explode and a seal shoot up, hang in the hair, squeal with what surely can only be delight and flop back in with a splash, it does make you wonder.

Particularly when they do it again and the squeal isn't any less delighted.

And again.

And again.

Next were the sharks. No apparent contentment here. Just menace. It's their eyes. And the teeth, obviously. But the eyes look mean. Painted-on mean. Even if the teeth could smile the eyes would still be looking at you with contempt. The background music at the shark tank doesn't do the sharks-aren't-mean-just-misunderstood lobby any favours either. It's sinister and dark, making the theme from *Jaws* sound like the soundtrack to *Finding Nemo*.

You can walk down and through their underwater home too, separated from the water by glass on three sides. The sharks cruise along looking for prey, which must be dispiriting because there isn't any. Here, they look fierce, efficient and deadly for no reason. Maybe that's why they look so mean, because they're pissed off that they spent so many millions of years evolving into perfect killing machines and now, in front of a daily paying audience, don't have any opportunity to show how good they are at it.

Sharks, however, are not the most dangerous creature in the sea. According to an information billboard the ocean's deadliest predator is, of course, humans, as a result of all the crap we put in it and all the good stuff we remove from it. So if you ever do bump into a shark outside the aquarium, just remember that you are more deadly than it is—and hope the shark knows.

Between the big tanks are lots of little ones that try to repli-cate the natural environment of each water creature, so that there is not only water in each one but bits of log and tree and natural habitat. At the aquarium they pride themselves on making the displays as natural as possible and seem to succeed. For example, at the platypus tank I spent five minutes looking and didn't see a single one. Just like in nature. How much more realistic can you get?

The visitors were young and old but there was virtually no one between eighteen and 30, presumably because when you are in that range you associate aquariums with school excursions and family outings, both of which are officially daggy.

Some visitors were so intent on getting every last thing on video that I doubt they saw a thing. Some even kept the camera to their eye as they made their way to the next display, pointing it to the floor to see where they were going.

The last display was the best, a Great Barrier Reef re-creation packed with a dazzling array of multi-coloured, shaped and sized tropical fish. This was the icing on the awe-cake. Everyone, babies to oldies, gaped in wonder. The fish looked back, utterly indifferent, which proves that people are far more interested in tropical fish than tropical fish are in people.

There were a few sharks in this giant tank, too. Cunning ones who had somehow managed to escape the shark tank and get to where the food was good? Yet they didn't appear interested. Perhaps they had been put in there to try and correct the impression the scary music had made in the shark tank, to show that some sharks really can live with other fish in peace. The fish looked nervous when they cruised past, though.

At the end of the reef tank there is a 3 metre by 6 metre window onto the reef display with room enough for people to sit and stare, which is what we did for I don't know how long. The view alone was worth the 24 bucks it cost to get in. It was dazzling.

Which meant that when we did leave it jarred to have to exit through the gift shop. Everywhere has one. They had one at the

Chinese Gardens too, but it was less intrusive. The aquarium gift shop jumps out at you like an escaped shark. The only way out is through it. Of course you can walk straight through and not linger, but the aisles are close together and I kept bumping into teatowels and coffee mugs. It would be far better to emerge directly into the Chinese Gardens to sit and contemplate what you had seen. But they have to have a gift shop so that every time you wash the dishes you can look at your Snub-nosed Dartfish teatowel and remember.

Past the gift shop is the snack bar. On the menu was fish and chips. It seemed wrong, like having giraffeburgers for sale at the zoo. I saw someone eating some and felt like calling the police.

After the fish, everything outside seemed grey by comparison. Even bright, colourful, shiny Darling Harbour. And especially work, which was where I was about to go. Before I did, we thought we'd complete the Darling Harbour experience with lunch at one of its eight trillion restaurants. But they all look designed to separate tourists and businessmen with expense accounts from their money, and have that way too expensive way of describing their food. Steak and chips becomes 'filet mignon in a poached apple sauce anointed with fragments of west Kenyan beetroot wearing a halo of pommes frites'. We gave the food a miss.

four

the wild man of manly

We took the next day off. If you can call lying in bed with food poisoning listening to drills, bobcats, loud radio and not-all-that-witty builder banter where every third word is 'fuckin' a day off. We prayed for rain or four o'clock, the only things that would make them stop.

It was the tuna curry. Good on Sunday, evil on Wednesday. Bibi lay on the bed watching us gradually dehydrate. It was like a scene from *Trainspotting*—two people vomiting with a baby lying between them.

By the end of the day the builders had gone home, we had lost all the weight we had to lose and were beginning to feel a bit better. Things were looking up. Bibi was sitting on Lucy, then she looked across at me and smiled. Then she vomited all over us.

On Saturday we heard voices over the back fence. It was Ivan, his architect and a third man, younger, with a shaved head. They were plotting and planning and pointing at bits of ground and talking about what would be there one day. Conversational fragments about walls and footings and various monetary figures drifted over. Eventually there was a knock on the fence and the third man's head appeared above it. He had a no-hands mobile phone that looked like the microphone helicopter pilots wear shoved in his ear and wrapping around to his mouth.

His name was Phil, he said, and he was the builder. He told us they wanted to put a pool in and asked us whether we would prefer it at ground level or halfway up the hill.

'How about halfway up the hill on our side?' I said.

He looked at me nonplussed for a moment, then laughed.

'I'll give you a quote,' he responded, calling my bluff.

I told him that if they really were asking our opinion, we'd prefer it on ground level. If we couldn't see it we'd get less jealous. One ridiculously hot day the previous summer we had visited friends who had just moved to Ryde. They were surrounded by pools they could see and hear but not touch. It was bad. They were having lots of cold showers and desperately trying to make friends with the neighbours.

'Sure,' Phil said with a smile. 'Whatever you'd like.'

Phil had been to builders' charm school.

The following Monday we went to Manly. Manly is what tourists think Australia is. One big beautiful beach, surrounded by just enough shops and places to stay to mean that if you do have to leave the beach for food, drink or shelter you don't have to go far, but not so many that it takes away from the focus of the place being a beach.

They know how to do a beach properly in Manly. It's very different from the eastern suburbs beaches. In the eastern suburbs, beaches always come as a surprise. You're in the middle of people and cars and houses and shops and wheelie bins and then suddenly you come round a corner and there's the beach. And next to it a carpark. In Manly you always know you're at the beach, even if you can't see it, in the same way you know it when you're on holiday somewhere small up or down the coast. It's a taste in the air, a particular shade of blue in the sky. Manly doesn't feel like a part of Sydney. It's as if you've fallen asleep at the wheel and accidentally driven 300 kilometres further north than you intended and ended up in a rapidly growing coastal town.

The beach is separated from the road by a pine tree-filled park with just enough picnic tables so that everyone who wants one gets one—and the shopping mall runs perpendicular to, not parallel with, the beach so that, unlike Bondi, the last thing you see as you launch yourself onto a wave isn't a row of shops.

At the other end of the mall is Sydney Harbour. Manly is at a point where the land narrows—from ocean beach to harbour is about 400 metres—before widening again to form North Head.

The first thing we saw when we got out of the car was a busload of Japanese tourists in their suits on the sand. It must be hard to have fun at the beach in a suit, but they were doing their best for the photographs. It wasn't just them in odd clothing, though. In early spring no one knows how to dress. A couple of warm days con us into thinking summer's on its way, but then a cold one follows and we're confused. So in early spring people hedge their bets. Walking along the beach was a man wearing black woollen pants and a tank top, another had on shorts and a jumper, and a woman wore a miniskirt, skivvy and sunhat. There was even a bare-chested bloke in Speedos, with a parka tied around his waist—wearing shoes and socks.

We loaded Bibi into the backpack and walked south along the beach. Most of the occupants were twenty-somethings with those deep, even tans that speak of months in the sun and yet look as though they somehow don't fit the persons they are on the outside of, as if it's the first time ever that their skin has been anything other than sickly pale. They may as well have carried signs saying 'European backpacker'.

At the south end, near the flags and the shops, a path has been cut into the base of the cliff, and we followed it. Along it little brass statues pop out of the rock. There is a long-nosed bandicoot, an octopus, even a body surfer. After five minutes we came to an ocean pool and sat on the rocks next to it looking out to sea. Behind us was the path, then a cliff that rose up to houses, and in front of us (to the north-east) 20 metres of rocks leading out to the ocean. If we looked a little further left we could see Manly Beach spreading out in a huge horseshoe north to Queenscliff. I don't know why looking at a big open view feels like it's doing you good, but it does. The view of sand and land and sea not only makes you forget you have a mortgage, it makes you forget what a mortgage is.

A bloke on a surf ski paddled toward us until, 20 metres from the pool, he stopped, stowed his paddle, rolled off the ski and swam over to the pool to do a few laps. The ski obediently waited, like Silver for the Lone Ranger. That's what I call getting a park.

We walked on another 15 minutes to tiny Shelley Beach, an oasis of underdevelopment tucked away on the north side of North Head, about 500 metres south of, and facing, Manly Beach. There's water then beach then park, and beyond is bush on three sides. The beach is calm, protected from waves, and some scuba divers were fully kitted up and ready to go. I suspect it was the first go for most because they kept finding ways to delay. Just when it seemed they were all ready, one would undo his wetsuit and fish around for something. When he'd finished another would realise there was something she had to check.

29

A bloke with a couple of dogs arrived and started throwing a tennis ball into the air at the water's edge. As the larger dog leapt for the ball, the little one, realising it had no hope of competing fairly, simply grabbed the big dog's tail in its teeth. Again and again the big dog would get itself ready to go flying into the air only to be jerked straight back to earth as soon as it took off. The ball would then hit it on the nose and bounce away. It must have been a Buddhist dog, because it didn't get angry with the little one—it just waited patiently for its owner (who, like everyone else, was laughing at it) to chuck the ball again so it could have another go.

When the owner accidentally threw the ball in the water the big dog dived in after it. But the ball had gone a couple of feet beyond the dog's depth and it obviously wasn't a swimmer. Lucy heroically hitched up her skirt and marched into the water to retrieve the ball.

'LUCY! YOU STUPID USELESS LUMP! GET IT!' shouted the dog's owner. Lucy wheeled round.

This was out of line. No one speaks to my . . .

'YOU'RE A WASTE OF SPACE LUCY, YOU'RE HOPELESS!'

'Now hang on. She's just . . .' I began.

'YOU ARE THE STUPIDEST DOG I HAVE EVER SEEN.'

Ah. I see.

'Excuse me mate,' I said. 'That woman who's getting the ball for you.'

'Yes?'

'Her name's Lucy, too.'

'Oh . . . sorry.'

He then went quiet.

A track led east up into the bush. We walked 100 metres along it and emerged at a cliff looking out to sea. Forty metres below waves crashed onto rocks. No scuba divers there. Turning right we headed south up a steep hill in the direction of North Head. Suddenly we were surrounded by real bush, not the pretend stuff you find in parks, but dense gum trees with branches and bushes and logs extending across the path. Within a minute we could see no evidence, apart from the track, that anyone else existed. It rose sharply, but Bibi was just the right weight in the backpack for the effort of carrying her to be enough to make me feel like I was a man, without being so heavy that it actually hurt.

I started to breathe deeply with effort. This was what I had been missing, the rejuvenating effects of the bush. The bush had been so accessible when I was growing up in Canberra and, via school trips and my parents' enthusiasm, I had spent many weekends in it. I was nineteen when I moved to Sydney and for the first few years would take every opportunity to get out to somewhere quieter. But living in the city eventually made it all seem too hard. Instead of a one-hour drive to get to the start of the walk, it was a one-hour drive to get to the edge of town. Gradually I left the city less and less, and the less you leave, the less you remember how good it feels to get out.

Ten minutes in a little bit of bush at Manly brought all the joy of it back to me. I felt as if I was rediscovering the bush, that every breath was freedom, even if I was only 100 metres from a beach and a café. I wanted to work hard and to see if I was up to it.

I pushed a branch away. This was what it was all about. When we got home I was going to suggest to Lucy that we sell up and move out of town, away from building sites and bitumen. Yes, she, who had grown up in Sydney and never lived anywhere else but Melbourne would blanch in horror, she would fight the idea, but in a few years when we were totally self-sufficient, and only came into town once a month to buy the latest organic fertilisers and new video games for Bibi, she would thank me.

I upped my pace. The path was steep, my heart was pounding and I could feel the sweat leaking into my eyes, but it felt good. I pushed another bush aside and strode on.

'WAAAAAA.' It was Bibi.

I turned around. That didn't help because she was on my back.

'WAAAAAAAA!'

'You hit her with a branch!' said Lucy.

I craned my neck back. Being used to parting branches for one, I had moved one just enough so that when it flicked back it had missed me comfortably but whacked Bibi a centimetre under her eye. There was a mark that she was trying to wash away by flooding it with tears, and trying to scare away with screams. In an instant my self-image deteriorated from wild bush man to that of horrible, irresponsible parent who'd almost taken his daughter's eye out with his carelessness.

We unloaded onto a seat at the top of the hill overlooking the ocean. Bibi made it clear apologies were not being accepted and that the only person she would take any comfort from was Mummy. I sat on the ground, ostracised, as Lucy worked her breast-feeding magic.

'Why don't you go and see what's up ahead?' said Lucy. The way she said it, it seemed what she really meant was that given I was such a bad father that I had nearly blinded our child, I should piss off and leave them alone.

'Fine.'

I stomped off up the track, into the trees again. Soon I couldn't hear or see them. It was just the bush and me. I had an overwhelming desire to just keep going, to run away. Behind was responsibility and duty, builders and nappies, pay cheques and bills. Ahead lay freedom, peace, and nature. The solitude of the track felt absolute. I wanted to be alone. I needed to be alone. I knew how Greta Garbo felt. Peace was freedom, and freedom was never having to answer to anyone. Once an only child, always an only child.

I increased my pace, and soon I was running along the track, sprinting past trees, ducking branches and hurdling logs. I would escape, I would run and run until I was free and then I'd build a tree house and live in it and hunt wild whatever-they-had-up-on-North-Head. Wild mosquito if I had to. I kept running, tore around a corner and ran smack into a stone wall. I bounced back. What was a 3-metre-high stone wall doing in the middle of a bush track on North Head? It ran in both directions for as far as I could see—obviously a message from God, put there to break my momentum and make me think. Did I really want to abandon all my responsibilities and become the mysterious wild man of Manly, living off berries and tourist scraps? Was God's wall suggesting that I should go back and try to be a good husband, father, employee and citizen? If so, why was there a hole at the bottom that looked just the right size for crawling through?

There was a sign above the hole: 'You are now entering Sydney Harbour National Park. No defined tracks exist beyond this point. Dangerous cliffs and gullies.' Underneath was a picture of a man falling off a cliff. I looked closer. No one I knew, thank God.

I crawled through the hole and walked on but my momentum had slowed. A drop of rain fell on my head. It was all very well to disappear into nature and become an enigma, but I should have brought a raincoat. And a good book to read. I slowed and stopped. I wasn't really cut out to be the wild man of Manly, and I didn't want to fall off a cliff. And if I did disappear into the bush never to be seen again, one day Bibi would find out that the last time I had been seen was just after she had started crying after I caused a branch to smack her in the face. She'd think it was all her fault and grow up wracked by guilt until one day it would all get too much for her and she'd run away into the bush to look for me and she'd get lost and it would all end in tears. I turned around, feeling noble. I may not need them, I thought, but they sure need me. I started walking back, secretly knowing that in fact it was the other way around.

five

powerful silvers

When we got home, next door was completely gone, carted away in skips. Ivan was sitting cross-legged on top of the final one, looking exhausted but vaguely satisfied. I wondered if we could ask him in for a cup of tea and a biscuit and persuade him to put in some grass, a swing, a slippery-dip and leave it at that.

Now at least things would be quieter. Building is a slower and more deliberate process than demolishing. Given that the demolishing had begun 3 metres from our bedroom, surely nothing to follow could match its noise. Week one was over. Things would now begin to improve.

I was wrong.

On Monday morning at 7 a.m. we were woken by smashing glass and bashing bricks. How the . . . what? Bibi wailed. What could they be knocking down? There was nothing left. The din seemed even closer and louder than before—but that was impossible because it had started right outside our window. The only way they could be closer was if . . . WAS IF THEY HAD STARTED ON OUR HOUSE! THE FIENDS! I leapt out of bed and raced to the window. Outside was . . . no one. Next door at number eighteen was a solitary labourer having a smoke. That couldn't be it, surely. Say what you like about cigarettes, but at least they're quiet.

Had I gone mad? Had I already become so conditioned to being woken by noise at 7 a.m. that even when it didn't happen my mind thought it had? Could you get conditioned to do that? In just a week? And not just me, but Bibi and Lucy too, because Lucy was staring about and Bibi was wailing again.

I heard another smash. The labourer took another puff. I staggered out the front door. Outside was a skip, a building truck and builders. Not outside number eighteen. Outside number twenty-two, the other half of our semi. They were at it too, and their first task, it seemed, was to start smashing away at our common wall.

We'd known it was coming. We just hadn't known when.

The owners were a thirty-something couple who'd bought the place after Dorothy died a few months before. Dorothy had lived in number twenty-two from age seven until her death at 84. Seventy-seven years. Since 1925. We had got to know her well, and she had told us stories about what Bondi used to be like: open spaces, big blocks, a quarry up the road and not a developer to be seen. She had lived with her parents and four siblings in the two-bedroom semi. In summer, two of the boys would sleep on the porch and in winter they would move into the lounge room. Now she was alone, long ago widowed and with no kids. Whenever she needed something she would rap on the common wall with her walking stick. She often called me in to replace light bulbs for her. Invariably, when I turned on the one she pointed out to test it, it would work perfectly. Dorothy would look at it in confusion as if it was playing a trick on her, but also with fear because she knew her mind was failing. It couldn't be a good grey zone to be in, being aware enough to know you were losing it.

She died in hospital quickly and left half her house to a distant relative and the other half to the church. That's right, the church. Who does that anymore? When the house was sold, Alan and Sarah moved in and it was obvious they were going to renovate. Dorothy's house looked like someone had lived in it for 77 years.

When you live next to a building site you know that it's going to be noisy, but you also know that it's not going to be noisy all the time. Building is a linear process; things have to be done in a particular order. Once demolition is complete, the footings have to be measured and dug. Then the bricks, scaffolding and sand have to arrive, then the bricklayers have to be ready. Along the way are all sorts of other jobs requiring various specialists that have have to be done in precisely the right order. Every contractor is juggling five different jobs and any delay by one of them stops the whole process. So we knew that the noise next door wouldn't be continuous. We'd get the odd day off. But two sites going, one either side, changed that. As I lay in bed staring at the ceiling and listening to the new builders smash away, I sort of knew that on any day when one site had a delay, the other would be going flat out.

We didn't just want to go to the places people usually go on Sundays, like Manly and Darling Harbour. We also wanted to explore suburbs we didn't know.

Haberfield is an inner-west suburb between Leichhardt, Five Dock and the harbour. It is full of lovely old free-standing Federation-style homes that reminded me of Adelaide, where my grandparents used to live. No semis, no flats, lots of verandahs. And it's quiet. There are the planes—it's under the flight path—but other than that, and despite being bounded by two of Sydney's busiest roads, Parramatta Road and Wattle Street, it's a bubble of quiet.

One reason it was quiet was that there was no building going on. In Bondi there were eight building sites within 100 metres of our home. In Haberfield we saw just one in three hours of wandering round, and even on that one no one was actually doing anything. It's a Federation suburb, which means that no one can alter the exterior of their house without the council being convinced that the changes will be in keeping with the character of the suburb. So you can't bung on a second storey or extend out the back unless the new bit is going to look as though it's been there from the start. In fact, you can't even paint your house without approval. In Haberfield a major development is putting a new flyscreen on the kitchen window.

The council also requires that a reasonable ratio is maintained between the size of the house and the total size of the block, which prevents the creation of the squashed look so common in Sydney. The suburb feels like a protected pocket from the fifties, a throwback to when men wore ties on the weekend and everyone on TV and radio spoke with those clipped, fake-sounding English accents. It's a suburb from a bygone era, from the deep distant past before everyone was obsessed with building. I bet all those TV shows about renovating rate badly in Haberfield. Jamie Durie could wander around unnoticed.

Haberfield is an architectural feast for the eyes and I was looking hard. Not the way you look about when you're walking on streets you've walked down hundreds of times before, but really looking, and really listening, like you do when you are overseas. Being in a suburb of Sydney you haven't visited before isn't as exciting as being in Paris, but it can still provoke curiosity, and even excitement.

The first person we met was a seventy-something lady standing out the front of her gnome-filled front garden. She was wearing a windcheater with a big 'Australia' on it which matched the flag in her front yard. The gnomes were obviously Australian gnomes.

As we wandered by she spied Bibi sitting on my shoulders.

'Ohhh! I could eat him,' she said.

We said 'Hello' but I kept a firm grip of Bibi's ankles in case she meant it.

'You're not from here, are you? Have you walked far?'

'No, we're just having a look around. We're from Bondi,' said Lucy.

'Ohhh!' she said as if Lucy's final word had been 'Saturn'.

She looked up at Bibi again. 'I could eat him.'

I know it doesn't matter if someone mistakes the sex of your child, especially if the child is under one. It's hard to tell from looks and Bibi was wearing a blue top. It's a perfectly under-standable mistake. But I had to correct her.

'She,' I said, 'she's a she.'

'Oh well,' she said, smiling all the wider, 'he's lovely anyway.' She looked up at Bibi. 'I want to gobble you up.'

Bibi apparently loved this idea, giggling hysterically. I made a mental note that at some point we'd have to explain to her to just say 'no' to cannibals.

Lucy also took the gender-bending to heart. Later that day, after I'd gone to work, she dressed Bibi up in knee-high pink socks so that no one could possibly fail to get the message she was a girl. The two of them hopped on a bus to Bondi Junction and the man in the next seat gave Bibi a huge smile then said, 'Hello, Mister Pink Socks!'

As we got nearer the centre of Haberfield it became clear that Joan of Arc is very big there. She has a church, a school and a retirement village all named after her. Why a retirement village? Surely the last thing you want as you near the end of your life, and look back at what you have and have not achieved, is to be constantly reminded of someone who changed the world before she turned nineteen. What a way to feel inadequate.

Perhaps the idea is to remind those occupants who otherwise might be tempted to feel sorry for themselves, as they witness the gradual decay of their minds and bodies, that they ought to at least be grateful they weren't burnt at the stake in their teens.

Despite all the beautiful Federation stuff, the architectural highlight of Haberfield is undoubtedly a house with a pillar on either side of the driveway connected by a miniature, to scale Sydney Harbour bridge. What a pleasure it would be to drive your car under the bridge each night. You'd feel like you were the captain of the *Fairstar*.

There are a lot of churches in Haberfield. Saint Joan's was the Catholic one and within 200 metres there were also Baptist, Anglican and Uniting, plus the Shalom Community Church, the name of which completely confused us. They were all lined up in a row like varieties of apple in a greengrocer's.

St Oswald's Anglican church had a sign outside it. There were ten lines in Korean, then two words in English: 'Young Couples', followed by a few more lines in Korean then two more English words: 'Powerful Silvers'. We guessed they were classes. Who 'Young Couples' were was obvious, but 'Powerful Silvers'? Presumably they are retirement village members trying to find their inner Joan of Arc. Silver is the new grey.

There weren't many people on the streets of Haberfield. I was used to the busy streets of Bondi filled with backpackers trying to work out the best way to waste the day, and unemployed actors, either alone checking their mobiles every

14 seconds to see if their agent had rung with the Big Offer or clustering in groups to reassure themselves that they weren't the only ones feeling desperate and alone. Pretty much everyone I had seen so far in Haberfield was old enough to live at the retirement village arm of Joan of Arc's Haberfield empire. I did spot one twenty-something bloke with a skateboard, but he seemed to know riding it outside the Baptist church would unleash *Footloose*-style reprisals and was carrying it as inconspicuously as he could. As soon as he crossed the suburb boundary at Parramatta Road he'd breathe a sigh of relief and jump on again.

It was only when we got onto the main drag, Ramsay Street, that the Italian presence in Haberfield became obvious and the place developed a bit of a buzz. Ramsay Street is full of cafés, barbers, real estate agents and cake shops.

We walked past the Quality Butcher (I always wonder if that's like when people say 'Okay, I'm going to tell you the truth now', protesting a bit too much) and a bit further on a jeweller's shop offering a Genuine Sale, presumably to differentiate it from all the other jewellers with fake sales on.

There was Ed Wilson Electrical, and right above it Ron Wilson Discounts. If the stuff Ron was discounting were the same electrical products Ed was selling, they'd have some frosty Christmases.

In the barber shop was a man being shaved with a cutthroat. A delightful relic of an era gone by, or just very lazy on the customer's part and a way of showing passers-by he had a bit too much time and money?

The chocolate shop was a world of its own, boasting work by talented choc-sculptors. The highlight was a chocolate toolkit, with a four-inch long chocolate screwdriver, pliers, spanner and hammer. It was beautiful in the way that normal screwdrivers, pliers, spanners and hammers aren't. The dilemma would be whether or not you could bring yourself to destroy the beauty by eating them. As if eating chocolate doesn't create enough guilt as it is, with these the eater would have to cope with the additional burden of destroying great art.

Atmosphere is a strange thing. You can break it down into components—appearance and number of buildings, landscape and people, friendliness of people, smiles per hectare—but in the end it's just there. Haberfield's atmosphere was friendly and unthreatening. It wasn't that of a suburb barely holding in check a manic exuberance and energy that could explode onto the streets at any moment (although I don't want to underestimate the excitement that the forthcoming St Joan of Arc's school fete, featuring 'pass the footy', a basket stall and jams was generating, and who knows what crazy things might happen if some of those powerful silvers turned up), but it felt nice to be there.

We entered a café at the corner of Ramsay and Dalhousie and it was Italian splendour. A glass counter full of cakes, the smell of coffee and a friendly bustle that was at odds with the quiet of the back streets. It could have been there unchanged for 50 years, apart from the television screen in the corner playing video hits. No one was looking at the screen, except in that zombie way you do when a television screen catches your eye. Why was it on? Why was it there? I feel the same way in train stations. Maybe I'll become a selective Amish, stringently opposed to not all but just some technological developments—public video screens, property development, concrete front fence/walls, leafblowers and car alarms.

I ordered the two unhealthiest-looking biscuity-cake things I could find and my first cup of coffee in ten months. I love coffee but have to give it up every year or so because I keep needing to increase my dosage to get the hit. I start by having one a day but inevitably soon get to the stage where if I don't have one by 11.07 a.m., another by 2.17 p.m. and a third by 5.45 p.m. the wheels fall off the wagon, and I become a head-achy grump who can only think about where my next cup is coming from. It's sort of like being a heroin addict except nowhere near as inconvenient, illegal, hard to give up or expensive. And you don't end up knicking your parents' DVD player.

My first cup in ten months was everything I had been dreaming about. Each sip seemed to increase tenfold my power to be exuberant, joyful, kind, compassionate, strong, loving and determined. Coffee is, however, a tragic example of the diminishing power of repetition. The first one in ten months makes me feel like Superman, the second like Batman and the third like only a slightly better version of myself. Before you know it, all that having one does is to allow me to stop thinking *Man, I need a coffee*, for a while. But for the time being I was riding the wave.

'It feels like being on holidays,' said Lucy.

It seemed ridiculous. We had driven for half an hour to a place we'd passed hundreds of times before and all we had done was walk around. What's more, my next stop was work. But Lucy was right. It was new, it was unfamiliar and we were exploring. While it would be wonderful to be exploring somewhere exotic like Rome or the Borneo jungle, the best part of exploring isn't being somewhere exotic, it's being somewhere new. New places pull you in through your senses, through your eyes and ears so that you become aware and alive. And we were somewhere new, even if it was only 10 kilometres from home.

I wondered if the secret to creating enjoyment was as simple as trying to ensure you continually had new experiences? Could feeding the senses a new dish of sights, smells and sounds each day be all that was needed to content and stimulate us? It couldn't be that easy. What if searching for new experiences itself became a habit? Would the fun wear off? Could going to new places and seeing new things become as routine as catching the bus to work? I once met an American in Indonesia who boasted that he had been travelling for eighteen months. He seemed cocky about it, but also bored. I told him I was going to see Mount Bromo, an active volcano, and asked if he wanted to come.

'Another active volcano? No thanks, I've seen plenty.'

I took another sip of my perfect, powerful coffee. Was it just the addictive stuff that got less fun the more you did it, or was it everything? Would the wonderful effect of the fish at the aquarium wear off if you worked there? Another day, another Snub-nosed Dartfish? Was anything exempt from this cruel law of diminishing returns?

Our month of Sundays was ostensibly about escaping the builders. But it seemed to me, as I sipped my coffee and felt my mind racing with nearly forgotten caffeine-induced power, that it might also serve another purpose—to try to learn how to enjoy each day as much as I could, to try to figure out how to be able to suck as much happiness out of each 24-hour period as there was on offer. It sounded simple, but I wasn't sure that it was.

At high school I had a friend called Matt who was a superman. He was in the first eight at rowing, the first fifteen at footy, he was the lead in the school play, captain of the debating team, tall, strong, in the top English and Maths sets, and a smart, funny, interested guy who hadn't let his success go to his head. Naturally he became school captain. At university he was a member of all the societies, still a super-sportsman, and was elected to the students' representative council. A lot of us wanted to be him.

When Matt finished university he worked for a law firm,

and in the next year he surprised us all in two ways. He stopped doing all the extra-curricular things he had always done and second, he came out. Looking back on it, he told me, he realised that keeping so busy was a strategy he'd adopted to stop himself from thinking about the fact that he was gay.

I had often thought that Matt had seemed intent on building the perfect CV, at creating a record of achievements that anyone would be impressed by. Everyone who knew him was impressed, but deep down he wasn't. Having gone through the initial angst, and eventual relief, of looking honestly in the mirror, he was happy to let the perfect CV sit, pretty much un-added to, from then on. He stopped being a superman, and became a real man.

He had learnt how to enjoy each day. And if you can do that, what else matters?

I, on the other hand, would never have said that the ability to enjoy each day as much as I could was one of my strengths. It was definitely one of Lucy's; she was excellent at it. Worries seemed to roll off her, and hassles and stresses passed over her like water over a rock. Bibi was pretty good at it, too. She, like most kids, was always totally engaged in whatever it was she was doing. If there was enjoyment to be had from something, she would get it.

But I spent too much time disengaged from what was hap-pening right now, thinking about either the future or the past. I clung possessively to worries—I wouldn't let them go—and I sponged up hassles and stress wherever I could find them. I was always preoccupied with where I was going and how I was going to get there, to the extent that what was happening right now got ignored. I had been that way since I was 25, which, ironically, is when I had finally got my act together.

At 25 I was a corporate lawyer, almost by accident. When I finished school I went to university because that's what everyone at our school did if they could, and I picked law because I didn't want to waste all those marks I had studied so hard to get. In my final year at law school everyone applied to all the big corporate law firms, so I did too.

I got a job at one of the biggest and corporatest. On my first morning they told me that to be good at the job I would need to read the *Financial Review* each day, and I immediately knew I was in the wrong place. The nearest I had gone to the business section of any paper was when I delved a little too deeply into the sports section and stumbled upon a page with company names and lots of numbers on it. The thought of working in a place where those names and numbers were important scared me. Everything thereafter reinforced the accuracy of my first impression, from the pressure not to leave the office each evening until it was too late to see your friends or your kids, to the work itself, which mainly involved helping lots of big companies make lots of money from each other.

Then it hit me, a blinding flash of inspiration that made sense of my whole life. I was a pathetic, stupid idiot. Of course. That was it. I had had every advantage anyone could ask for—born to nice, upper middle-class parents, private school, university education—but because I had drifted mindlessly along without ever thinking about what it really was that I wanted to do I was in completely the wrong place. All I, too, was doing was building a CV, albeit one considerably less exciting than Matt's, to impress others.

I realised that if I kept refusing to steer the ship one day I would be a 55-year-old corporate lawyer who drank too much, tried to crack onto his secretary and drove a fast red car that caused everyone to make jokes behind his back about his penis size. I suddenly saw that I had wasted most of my life doing the wrong thing. It gave me a shock, and it finally got me off my arse.

That's when I started to work out where I wanted to be, and how I would get there. Which was all very well, in that it motivated me to get out of corporate law and into an area I found far more interesting and satisfying, criminal law, and to kick-start a stand-up comedy career that I had previously been too scared to have a go at. But I over-compensated. I changed from never thinking about where I was going at all, to thinking about it all the time. I became totally goal-focused, and was always looking for angles and trying to work out how to create, and take advantage of, opportunities. So much so that without really noticing it I lost the ability to enjoy the ride. I was so focused on tomorrow, I forgot about today.

Ten years on, most of the destinations I had aimed at had been reached. I had the job I wanted, I was living with the woman I wanted and we had the baby we both wanted. So why wasn't every part of every day a joy? Why couldn't I switch the planning part of my brain off, chill out and enjoy things? Why did I spend so much of the present, so much of my time with Lucy and Bibi, distracted and half-absent, wondering about something that might or might not happen next week?

'Do you want to get going?' said Lucy.

Just as I had been doing. Here we were, sitting in a café having a holiday, and I was mentally off somewhere else again. Surely a first step towards enjoying each day as much as I could was to actually be in each day as much as I could, really be in it, and clearly I had a bit of work to do on getting better at that. But at least sitting in a café in Haberfield I had realised for the first time that enjoying each day as much as I could was a good aim to have.

I looked up at Lucy. 'Sure.'

I also realised that I hadn't been plotting or planning before we stopped to have coffee. I hadn't been worrying about tomorrow, but simply enjoying the newness of wandering around and looking at things I'd never seen before. I felt strangely exhilarated, as if some new way of looking at life had been revealed to me. I looked down at my empty cup and hoped it wasn't just the coffee.

Although it had been a wonderful morning, we did manage a disagreement over the route of return. Lucy wanted to go past more shops whereas I preferred back streets.

'This is like a three-legged race,' she said.

Again she was right. We could do whatever we wanted as long as we both agreed on what it was. That's what travelling with someone else is, even if it is only in four-hour stints. It involves lots of new and exciting decisions to make, hence lots of new and exciting ways in which to disagree. Luckily Bibi was too small to have an input, or we would have been split three ways.

Lucy and I had discovered early in our relationship that we had dissimilar travelling styles. After we had been together about a year we went to Europe for a month, first stop Rome. The first two days were full of little compromises, me waiting outside while she looked in a clothes shop, then her not looking in the next clothes shop because she didn't want me to have to wait outside again. On the third day we went to the Forum, a huge area of ancient Roman ruins. I wanted to race around, to walk and walk and soak up as much as I could, and kept forcing myself to slow down to accommodate Lucy's saunter. She, of course, was hurrying up to accommodate me, but I didn't notice that.

Eventually, inevitably: 'Come on, let's go up here.'

'In a minute.'

'We've been here five minutes already.'

'You go then.'

'What?'

'I'll meet you back at the hotel in, say, three hours.'

'Wha . . . but?' It didn't fit the image. We were young lovers joined at the hip, strolling around the Holy City arm in arm, every moment a joy and even momentary separation unthinkable. That was the movie I wanted to be in. If we went our separate ways it would mean . . . what would it mean?

I tried to explain. 'But . . . what if . . . I don't have a watch.' Very feeble.

'Ask someone the time. Bye.'

It saved the holiday, perhaps more. Each morning we'd break up for a few hours and explore on our own, meet back at the hotel for lunch, laze about and then head off together in the late afternoon.

In Haberfield we remembered the Forum and compromised on half the shop street and half the back street. It felt very adult.

Halfway back to the car we stopped and talked to a seventyish man lingering outside his house, arms resting on his front fence. He wasn't a fan of Haberfield's 'stupid heritage stuff' and lamented the fact that he had to ask the council 'before I can paint the bloody letterbox'.

'Ah well,' I said, 'at least you don't have developers building everywhere.'

'Might as well have, what with all the noise from the buses and planes.'

We paused. And listened. Crystal-clear silence.

'It's not as bad as it used to be,' he eventually said begrudgingly.

'Bye,' he said as we moved on. 'I'm just waiting here for the mailman, then I'll be back inside. He's late today.'

We made our way back to the car along Crescent Street

which, strangely, at that point seemed to be dead straight. As we drove out of Haberfield I thought about that old bloke. If the mailman arriving was a big event there couldn't be much else going on. I hoped he got some letters—and not just bills.

six

a bit of east in the west

That night when I got home from work, I was greeted by a sight that made my blood freeze. A shopping trolley was standing outside our house. (Or should that be sitting outside our house? Anyway, it was there.) I had seen the shopping trolley hanging around outside number eighteen for a couple of weeks. That was okay; it was number eighteen's business. Now, it was outside our house.

For some reason it made me incredibly angry. It was obviously the builders' doing. How dare they, after waking us up each morning and blocking our light and driving us bonkers with their drills, put a shopping trolley outside our house. I grabbed it and shoved it back along the footpath until it bashed into a pile of rubble outside number eighteen. So there. No one fucks with me.

The next morning the trolley was there again, directly outside our front gate. I looked over at number eighteen. None of the builders giggled or looked guilty. They said good morning as normal, but I *knew* one of them had done it.

We got in the car and drove off somewhere peaceful and stress free. Auburn and Lakemba.

I had driven past Auburn many times over the years but had never thought of going in. This time we turned off the Western Distributor and headed south along St Hilliers Road. We soon came to its major intersection with Boorea Street. Across the road was Auburn. Luckily the lights were red because it gave us a chance to let the view sink in.

Across the intersection at ground level was a row of modest weatherboard houses. Towering above them, looking as if it was growing out of their roofs, was the Auburn Mosque. On 4000 square metres stood a huge grey central dome, big enough to hold 5000 people, flanked by two towering minarets—or spires—reaching to the sky. It looked like the gateway to the suburb. It was grand, impressive and slightly intimidating.

All I knew about Lakemba and Auburn was that a lot of Arabs lived there, a lot of Muslims lived there, each suburb had a mosque and whenever there was a news story about Muslims in Sydney the media went there for comment and footage. And that driving toward it made me feel slightly uneasy.

I, of course, am a supporter of multicultural Australia who believes that in times of international suspicion it is even more important than usual to reach out and build bridges between people, and to focus on the common humanity that connects us all, no matter what we look like, where we are from, who we believe in and whether or not we play cricket. I believe that it is wrong to make fun of anyone because of their race, unless of course they are from England, America or New Zealand, in which case it is okay because they speak English and look like me. I understand that when we feel threatened it is far easier to label a group of people who are different as the villains (the rich, the unions, the Muslims, the dole bludgers, the Catholics, the Jews, the hairdressers) than it is to actually puzzle our way toward the truth, but I believe that puzzle our way toward the truth is what we must nevertheless do.

I had always felt nothing but contempt for racist attitudes, either overt or subtly betrayed, such as the caller I once heard on talkback radio who began a spray with, 'Look, don't get me wrong, I'm no racist. Like, I really like Thai food an' that, but . . .'

In short, I believe all those things that broad-minded, educated people are supposed to believe—that we should open our arms and embrace, rather than fear, difference. So why did driving to the Muslim centre of Sydney make me feel slightly uneasy?

Because while I believed that we should open our arms and embrace, rather than fear, difference, I had never actually done it. It wasn't as if I had actively avoided it. It was just that I had never seen much difference to embrace.

I grew up in Anglo middle-class Canberra and was insulated from diversity even further by attending Canberra Grammar School, where the students were so starved of proper minorities to have a go at they had to tease me for being Irish, a label which in my family's case was 120 years out of date.

The university I attended, Sydney University, was back then very Anglo and very middle class. The closest I got to a multi-cultural experience there was going to nearby Newtown for a kebab.

Since I'd lived in Sydney I'd lived in Anglo middle-class Crows Nest, mainly Anglo middle-class Glebe, and Bondi, where my main connection to the large multicultural popula-tion was being woken up by pissed English backpackers singing outside our window at 3 a.m. as they stumbled back to the hostel. I had, of course, preached about how wonderful multi-cultural Australia was at Anglo middle-class dinner parties, but as we drove gradually west to Lakemba and Auburn it occurred to me that I knew jack shit about multicultural Australia. The closest I had ever really got to it was ringing the local Thai restaurant and asking for a number 64 with chicken, a number 26 with seafood, and two boiled rice.

The picture before us as we entered Auburn was of two cultures. The bottom half was Anglo Western Sydney, the top half Middle Eastern Sydney. Together they were Auburn, and Lakemba, and all the other places where East and West bump up against each other. I wondered how much, if at all, they had merged to produce some sort of cultural fusion. Or were the two parts, as the image we could see from the traffic lights suggested, on each other's doorstep yet separate, trying as best they could to pretend the other didn't exist?

The lights changed. We drove into Auburn and immediately saw a very different image. In a busy park Muslim girls in *hijab* (veils) were playing soccer with Arabic, Asian and Western boys. There's your cultural fusion. Kids; they just don't know enough to be paranoid and afraid.

We parked near the shops. It's got a hum, Auburn. There are busy, buzzy streets with lots of people about. It's a big centre with lots of butchers. Every third shop is a butcher, and one of the other two is a tobacconist. If you smoke and eat meat, it's the place for you. One day the shops will merge and sell lamb cigarettes and roll-your-own-chicken breasts.

We passed Michael's Smoke Zone, and a pharmacy that looked like any other in Sydney apart from its name, the Ramadan Pharmacy. Western culture doesn't mix religion and business like that. There are no Lent Newsagents or Jesus Died On The Cross Milk Bars. Western culture generally keeps religion in its own box, separate from the rest of life and away from commerce, an approach which runs the risk of making religion irrelevant. Almost everyone my age I know was brought up Christian but gradually drifted away as they lost any sense of connection between what the church was on about and their own lives.

We passed Australian Bizarre Bargains, but they only sold electrical goods so how bizarre could the bargains be? A bizarre bargain isn't letting a TV go for $80, it's selling one for four paintbrushes and a slug. So much for truth in advertising.

Outside a dress shop two Arabic men were talking about how to get New Zealand permanent residency if you were Iraqi. Inside was a tiny sky-blue dinner suit with huge black bow tie fitted onto an eight-year-old boy-sized mannequin. No wonder there's trouble in the world when parents exist who make innocent children wear such things.

Next door was a beautician that promised to create 'hair of elegance'. An Arabic woman walked in but I doubted they could help her. Her hair was impossibly elegant already.

Another example of two cultures side by side—a Muslim woman in a *hijab* walked past a giant billboard featuring a woman with pretty much nothing on, advertising power drills or chips or lawnmowers or something. Western culture may have separated religion from commerce, but sex is still right in there.

We passed a clothing shop where a sign politely requested that we 'please do not steal', and obeyed it. Most of the shop signs were in both Arabic and English, and most faces on the street were Arabic or African. There were more men than women, which would be unusual most other places on a weekday.

A park next to the railway line was full of kids playing and not-quite-relaxed parents keeping a watchful eye. Next to the swings was a shopping trolley. Not our one, I hoped. It'd be really spooky if it had followed us. Near the road was a big rock commemorating the opening of the park in 1985. The plaque listed all the Auburn councillors of the day, and back then all thirteen had Anglo names. When I got home I looked up Auburn Council's website. Their slogan is 'Many Cultures, One Community' and judging from the names and photos they now have five Anglo, three Asian and three Arabic councillors.

The mayor's page on the website indicated that in the last few months the council had formed a partnership with the NSW Service for the Treatment and Rehabilitation of Torture and Trauma Survivors, which provides services to refugees settling in New South Wales. It had also held a soccer benefit match to support Refugee Week, and had invited nominations from the community to select the best places to put up four council Christmas trees. Many Cultures, One Community.

We passed what looked like the world's most elaborate Turkish delight shop, the contents of which looked so good that I almost forgot I don't like Turkish delight, and followed the railway line away from the shops toward the mosque. On the way we passed several newly built and nearly built apartment blocks, the first fully concreted non-carported front garden we had seen, and the Sydney–Turkish Welfare and Cultural Centre.

The Auburn Gallipoli Mosque is on North Parade, just a couple of hundred metres from the shops. As we got closer it became obvious we had arrived at a significant time. It was midday Friday, and lots of people were coming to the mosque. The streets were full of parked and parking cars.

The mosque was just as impressive and imposing up close. Surrounding the huge dome were the Islamic equivalent of verandahs, fountains and grassy bits. There were dozens of places outside to sit or stand and talk, which is what many were doing. And just 10 metres away were the weatherboard houses.

At the fountain, people gathered and removed shoes. We could see several hundred people outside, more through the doors inside, ranging from teenagers to 80-year-olds. Unlike almost all Christian churches, the congregation included a lot of 18-year-olds, 25-year-olds and 33-year-olds. Islam did not seem to have misplaced a generation in the same way Christianity had.

'What a mix,' I said.

It took Lucy to point out the obvious. 'Except women.'

She was right. Midday on Friday at the mosque was man-time. She also noticed something I had never seen poking out from a suburban church—security cameras.

I wondered about the time. Christians and Jews have times for worship that don't interfere with the working week. It couldn't be easy, especially in Sydney, to ensure work commitments didn't interfere with worship time on a Friday. Perhaps it is an indication of differing priorities. Rather than give matters spiritual a low priority and fit religion in around other things, perhaps more Muslims are committed to giving the spiritual side of life a higher priority and fitting work and other things in around it.

Though all we did was walk past the mosque as the crowd gathered, I had a sense of intruding, perving, of being somewhere I didn't belong, looking at things that were none of my business. Yet I can't say where I got it from. No one looked at us with hostility. No one looked at us at all. It was more an indication of my own uneasiness at being there than of anything else. Perhaps in the past year I'd read too many stories about gangs of 'men of Middle Eastern appearance'. I think I half-expected them to be prowling around. But this wasn't a gang, it was a group coming together to worship.

We made our way back to the car, still passing men heading

towards the mosque, and then to Lakemba. Lakemba is 15 minutes' drive south-east of Auburn. We turned off Punch-bowl Road and parked in Wangee Road, a semi-main road flanked by drab grey apartment blocks.

It's funny how big the difference between theory and practice can be. As we started to walk in the general direction of the shops a woman wearing the all-covering *burka* walked past, and for all my talk and thought over the years about accepting others my first thought was not of similarity, but of difference. Whereas in my own street I might have felt secure enough to smile and say 'hello', here, in unfamiliar territory, I stared, thought *don't stare*, looked away, stared again and looked away again. Just because I'd never seen a pair of eyes behind a veil walking down my street.

There wasn't much happening on Wangee Road. Washing flapped from apartment balconies and there was a lot more concrete than grass. It's not rundown, but it's not pretty either, and trees are rare. As we got closer to the shops we passed a dental clinic and a Lady Doctor. Then a dentist. Then a dental clinic. And another one. Eight separate dentists within 200 metres. Just as Auburn does smokes and meat, Lakemba does teeth. Eleven dentists in the suburb. Bondi has cafés, Crows Nest restaurants, Lakemba dentists. Has the idea that people of the same ethnicity live in the same area spread to jobs? Doctors in Pymble, stockbrokers in Vaucluse, dentists in Lakemba.

Between the dentists were Lebanese cafés, second-hand electrical stores and agents, both travel and real estate. Most faces in the street were Arabic, as were most of the shops, but the buzz that brought Auburn alive was missing. There were fewer people about, and they were doing less more slowly, as if everyone who had any energy had nicked off to Auburn or somewhere else. There's no excess money in Lakemba, in the people or the shops. No one was flashing it about, dressing up rich or driving a fast car.

The closest Lakemba got to having a gang were groups of middle-aged to elderly Arab men sitting outside cafés sipping dark coffee. No women with them. In fact there were very few couples in the street. Men yes, women yes, but not together and never holding hands. A couple of the men looked at us as we passed, and I felt conspicuous. I could imagine them being there every day, just like the men at Bronte. A government program should be set up to get them to swap for a day, although the Bronterians might look a tad underdressed in the middle of Lakemba wearing Speedos.

I think I'd been expecting to see lots of young, tough-looking men hanging around or cruising laps in cars that were more stereo than engine. In fact there weren't many young men about at all—maybe they were all at work—and we only heard one car playing doof-doof music, and it just drove right on through. In Bondi they do laps.

Most shop signs were in both Arabic and English. Orient Travel offered trips to Beirut twice a week, and boasted that 'We Speak Australian'. A real estate agent was selling 'A Bit of East in the West!' The unintended irony of the slogan was that it described the entire suburb; a bit of the Middle East in the west of Sydney. It also, in a very different way, described me. A bit of Sydney's east visiting the west. Out of place.

In the middle of the shops was that part of any suburb where you can always find Anglos—the pub. It, too, looked out of place. I stood outside it and looked down the street. About 40 people, five of them Anglo. Then inside. Sixteen people, all Anglo. *Vive la différence.*

'Don't take notes so obviously,' Lucy whispered. As usual I was jotting things down as we walked.

'Why not?'

'Because you look nosy.'

'Oh, come on.'

'You do. It's intrusive. People might not like it.' We were arguing in whispers.

'You never said that in Manly,' I said, 'or Haberfield.'

She looked at me, and the unspoken comment was, well, this isn't Manly or Haberfield. This is Lakemba, and she felt uncomfortable.

I wanted to scoff, but I felt uncomfortable too.

But was it us or was it them? How much anxiety had we brought with us? How much of it was our own baggage, our own fears, our own reaction to the media blitz associating Muslims and 'things to be feared'? It was all very well to talk about being open-minded, but harder to actually be so.

Atmosphere is not just about the place and the people who are there. It's also about the relationship between those two things and the observer. If you go to Paris and fall in love, you'll probably like the city a whole lot more than if you go there and break up with your partner, lose your watch and have computer trouble. But it's the same Paris.

We veered onto the back streets. Once we got a block or two away from the shops, apartment blocks gave way to comfy middle-class houses. We hadn't got to the mosque yet but we did see other indicators of community that undermined the idea of a nearly exclusively Muslim suburb: an Anglican church, a Uniting church, a Seventh-Day Adventist church and a Masonic centre. Even a Boy Scout hall. I bet there was a gang in there every Thursday night shouting out strange slogans and tying weird knots.

We wound our way back past the car to the mosque. The Lakemba mosque, the Imam Ali Mosque, is also huge and can hold thousands. It is flat-roofed with one minaret rising above it. We saw two men walk in the front, then a woman in full *burka* with only her eyes showing disappeared into the carpark underneath.

Thirty metres down the road was a man sitting out the front of his flat on a little brick fence watching the world go by. I said hello, he smiled back and we talked about the weather and Bibi for a while. He was the only person we talked to in Lakemba and he was English. Then I realised he was also the only person I'd smiled at and said g'day to.

For every image of difference in Auburn there seemed to be a corresponding one of acceptance. In Lakemba I felt like a nosy tourist coming to spy, which is what I was. And like a nosy tourist, I didn't stay long enough to really get to know the place. I stayed just long enough to get nervous about the difference.

But if I felt out of place and conspicuous in Lakemba, how then do those who live there feel outside of Lakemba? What sort of vibes would the veiled Muslim woman I had gawked at feel if she walked down the streets of Parramatta, Manly or Burwood? How did she feel when people like me stared at her? At least when I felt like an outsider I had the security of knowing I was part of the cultural, religious and ethnic majority.

I resolved then not to stare anymore. Not even accidentally. Not at Muslims, not at Africans, not at the disabled, not at people who had a bit of parsley stuck between their teeth. But I knew I still would. So I made a second, more realistic resolution. That when I did stare I'd smile as well.

seven

obsession

That night when I got home the trolley was still out the front of our house. I pushed it back in front of number eighteen. If it had even a rudimentary consciousness it would have been confused. The next morning it was back in front of our place again, with a loaf of mouldy bread in it. Were the builders upping the ante by sending back a loaded trolley?

Our response would be vital.

I went inside and, over the banging from both sides, shouted to Lucy. 'Let's vomit in it.'

Lucy raised half an eyebrow. It's something very few people can do and it has a particular meaning that approximates to, 'What a novel idea. It is entirely without merit.'

'Then they'll think we ate the bread and we got sick. They'll feel guilty.'

This time the eyebrow went right up. Then she went back to her magazine.

'I'll do it,' I shouted over the drilling, knowing I wouldn't.

She didn't even look up.

I fussed about for a bit, then went out the front again to see exactly how mouldy the bread was and what sort of loaf it had been. I don't know why. I carried Bibi in my arms to elicit as much sympathy for myself from myself as I could. I opened the front door and saw they had struck again.

This time it was number twenty-two. Some time in the last ten minutes one of them had nailed a metre-long Masonite plank to the top of our adjoining fence. It wasn't in my way, but I was outraged. How dare they do it without asking. Just to show them I wasn't someone they could simply walk all over and expect no retribution from, I grabbed it, broke off a tiny corner and threw it at their stupid house. The wind caught it and it blew away. I looked at the plank. No visible difference, really. I looked at Bibi. I think we both knew I'd made my point.

I slammed the door loud enough to almost hear it over the drilling. As I stomped down the hall it occurred to me that it was all very well to pat myself on the back for having been able to enjoy myself on a four-hour holiday in Haberfield after turbo-charging up with coffee, but that when it came to trying to maintain peace of mind when things weren't perfect I still had a way to go.

But I wasn't as bad as I used to be.

In 1996 I was working as a lawyer for legal aid, and had been since 1994. I worked at various local courts around Sydney representing pretty much anyone who turned up and satisfied three criteria: they had been charged with a criminal offence; they didn't have a private lawyer; and they didn't have much of an income. Since I joined legal aid I had represented people charged with shoplifting, assault, armed robbery, drug possession, drug supply and even murder.

Each day I met people with fucked up lives. Of course they were all, to a large degree, responsible for that themselves. But almost invariably, when I asked a few questions of a client, a history of a disjointed and unpleasant childhood would emerge. Typically he (and it was 'he' about 90 per cent of the time) would have a history of receiving violence from one drunken parent and indifference from the other, drug addicted one—if they had contact with both, that is.

I had grown up having no understanding of why anyone would take heroin, but when someone explained to me that it was the ultimate pain-killer, I slowly started to get it. And I began to understand how lucky I had been to be born into comfortable middle-class circumstances to parents who were good to me.

When I say I began to understand, I mean that in a purely intellectual way. I understood how emotional pain can motivate short-term pain relief through drugs such as heroin, and how that can lead to addiction and that can lead to crime. I reasoned how all this could happen, and I tried to display empathy with my clients without being a complete wet blanket. My primary job was to give them legal advice and representation, but sometimes it was also to try and help in a more holistic way. My message to clients became, 'Shit happens and it's probably happened to you, but in the end it's up to you—and only you—what you do about it.'

But I remained an outsider. It wasn't my world. I came into it at 8.30 each morning and left it again at 5. Which was a good thing.

Occasionally something crossed over emotionally. Once I represented a young woman who was probably mildly intellectually disabled and who had a late-night job packing shelves. It was pretty lonely work, and to pass the time she had started to eat the odd chocolate bar. Then another one, and perhaps a packet of snakes as well. As the weeks went by she kept eating and eating, and eventually she had effectively stolen a thousand dollars' worth of merchandise from her employer. At court she was terrified, as was her mother. She'd never had her daughter assessed to see whether she was intellectually disabled—but she referred to her daughter as her 'special' one. The whole thing was very sad. The magistrate saw it that way too, and put the girl on a good behavior bond, effectively ending the case. But driving home I couldn't get the image of her frightened face out of my head and had to pull over because I was crying.

Over the next few moths I'd think of her and wonder why. Mainly though, I did what they tell you to do, and what you make yourself do automatically—I distanced myself. And I had another focus, my comedy career.

It is obvious now that doing gigs three nights a week and trying to find more time to write, on top of working full-time, was running me down, and that creeping exhaustion played a part in what was to come. But at the time I was oblivious. Perhaps I sensed that I was so busy rushing from one thing to another I didn't have time to actually enjoy anything. But if I did sense it, it didn't seem important.

One day I had a coffee with a friend, Steve, another criminal lawyer. We swapped work stories as you do, and Steve told me how someone in a case he was involved in had claimed that Steve had tried to pressure him into changing what he was going to say in court. Steve wasn't a person who would ever do something like that and, as he was acting for a client who was broke, he certainly would have had no financial motivation to do anything inappropriate. But someone had phoned Steve later and told him he was being investigated for attempting to influence a witness, a very serious offence that could lead to a jail sentence.

'When was that?' I asked

'Um … 'bout six months ago.'

'And what happened?'

'Nothing.'

'Nothing?'

'Never heard back from them.'

'You must have been terrified,' I said.

'It did scare the crap out of me at first,' he replied, 'but after a while I forgot about it.'

'Forgot about it!?' The idea of forgetting about something so potentially earth-shattering seemed bizarre to me.

'Yeah, something new to worry about must have come up.' He laughed.

I didn't. I felt shaken. I had never thought about this dangerous side of being a criminal lawyer before. If something like this could happen to Steve, then surely it could happen to me.

I started asking fellow lawyers if there had been a time when they, too, had almost been sucked into a case. Many of them had a similar story. It seemed that if you were a criminal lawyer for long enough, it was almost inevitable that at some point someone would make a complaint about you.

And then somehow, instead of shrugging my shoulders and getting on with it, I started to become obsessed with the idea that sooner or later someone would make an allegation about me. I had always gone out of my way to be completely above board in every way, but I couldn't stop thinking about how many one-on-one conversations I had to have as part of my job, and how easy it would be for someone to try and get me into trouble. I started to get very paranoid.

I started playing mental tapes of every work-based con-versation I'd ever had and wondering which was the one that was going to get me into trouble. I started thinking about it all the time. And the more tired and run down I got, the more I thought about it. I became obsessed with the idea that something terrible was going to happen to me and spent hours imagining what it would be in ridiculous detail. Looking back on it, I somehow lost control of my mind. It started to spend all its time in places that were very unpleasant indeed.

Whenever I had free time I would spend it worrying. I ran through every possibility. What if, in that case three weeks ago, someone accused me of this? What if it was some other case? The police could be on their way to see me now. They could be. Maybe they weren't, though. Maybe someone had made a complaint about me and it was in a pile somewhere and next Tuesday, or the following Wednesday, or the Thursday after that, someone would read it and come to see me. Or maybe not. The possibilities went around and around and around. My thoughts were an exhausting, repetitive worry-loop, trying to anticipate events I couldn't control and which, in fact, didn't exist. It seemed unfair. I had worked hard over the past few years to get away from being a miserable corporate lawyer, to get going in two jobs I enjoyed. I seemed to be getting somewhere and now, all of a sudden, it all seemed vulnerable. From feeling completely safe I had somehow thought myself into a position where I was imagining, with terrifying intensity, something going very wrong. And it wasn't even because I had a guilty conscience. I hadn't done anything wrong. What was going on?

It's not unusual for someone to occasionally feel that the shit might hit the fan. But what usually happens is that when time passes and it doesn't, you gradually relax. But I couldn't. As each day passed I worried with even more intensity, using every spare moment to think up new ways that someone, somewhere, could bring about my downfall.

It started to get absurd. Initially my fear might have been useful as a wake-up call to ensure that I triple-checked everything I did and never put myself in a position where I was vulnerable. But as the days went by I continued to obsess about getting in trouble somehow. It's a great thing, the human brain, but mine turned against me. It ignored logic and would not, could not, stop worrying about something that wasn't going to happen.

What if, what if, what if . . .

It became the first thing I thought about every morning and the last thing I thought about at night. I thought about it on the bus, at work, when I was out. I thought about it when I woke up at 4 a.m. for a piss. I thought about it when I was on stage doing stand-up. My mind would go rushing around the familiar tracks again while my mouth switched to auto pilot. I became adept at carrying on conversations with just half my brain involved, as the other half continued the seemingly vital task of racing down and around all the scenario paths. It always seemed that if I could just think about it a bit more, just think it through one more time, I'd be able to work out a way of proving to myself that nothing could go wrong. But I never quite could.

If I caught myself not worrying, it was as if I had let my guard down. There seemed to be safety in worry—it meant I was preparing myself as best I could, that I had my guard up so that if something did happen, at least I would have done my best to anticipate it.

Sometimes it occurred to me that I had a higher risk of getting cancer than of getting into trouble and yet that was no help. I'd never been near cancer, so at some basic level I didn't really believe that cancer could ever threaten me. It was far away.

In retrospect, my obsessive worrying was a way of trying to exert control over something outside my control. Endlessly trying to anticipate every possible sequence of events was less scary than accepting there were things that I didn't know and events that might affect me that I couldn't do anything about.

The fact that a part of me knew this was an inevitable risk of being a criminal lawyer and that all my colleagues faced it too, and that getting in trouble was very unlikely, didn't help. But it did, unfortunately, make me too embarrassed to talk to any of my fellow lawyers about it and get them to help me analyse the possibilities in a realistic and logical way. I thought that if I did, they'd think I was crazy. Which in a way I was—I knew I was over the line of rational anxiety into crazy doom fantasyland, but knowing it didn't help.

What I should have done then was quit, or gone on long term leave. But most of the job I liked, it was what I wanted to do and leaving would feel like failure. My life looked like a good one and even though the man at the centre of it was having the worst time of his life, he was dammed if he was going to let anyone know.

From the outside my life looked the same. I got up in the morning and went to work, I lived with Lucy and I worked as a stand-up comedian two or three nights a week, persuading people that their everyday lives were full of hilarious things to laugh at. Sometimes when I was at work or out, I had to sneak away to the toilet for five minutes, just to sit down one more time and think through all the possibilities, to get them straight in my head. It was like an addiction, but without the good bits. But I never missed any sort of work commitment. I don't think anyone I didn't tell—and I told very few people—ever knew there was anything wrong. Friends and workmates might have thought I was a bit quiet, but nothing more. Years of stand-up had taught me how to project calm and confidence even when I didn't feel it.

But I felt for all that time as if the most important part of my life had been taken away—the part where I enjoyed things, where I had fun, laughed and thought it was good to be alive. It wasn't there any more. I was swamped by fear.

I missed one social commitment, a friend's Saturday birthday lunch. I lost it at home an hour before we were due. I was sobbing, overwhelmed at how I had so quickly and conclusively lost control of my life. I remember realising that I seemed to have lost the capacity to feel joy. It was gone and life had become something to endure, a storm to be waited out. So we didn't go. Another time Lucy and I were in David Jones at Bondi Junction, buying our first whitegood together, when I became overwhelmed, and started trembling as I held a blue kettle. We didn't buy it. I stopped reading detective stories, because any reference to courts or police would get me going. But I stayed a lawyer. All the work I did I triple-checked, and I made sure I protected myself from any unlikely way in which things could go wrong.

Occasionally I mentioned my nagging fears to someone, and they would always give me the same sensible but impossible-to-follow advice: Just forget about it.

Eventually I saw a counsellor, a sensible and understanding woman who looked like Cher. She suggested I carry in my wallet a card with the word 'STOP' written on it, and whenever I got into my anxiety loop take it out and look at it. She said that if I did this I'd feel better within a couple of days. It didn't work.

I tried a kinesiologist. She read my innermost thoughts by poking and prodding me and asking me to push my hand against hers. She told me it was clear that I had a problem with my relationship with my father. I told her that maybe I did, but that it was nothing compared with the problem I had of obsessively worrying about the possibility of getting into trouble. She told me that I should think of the worst possible thing that could happen, then embrace it and look for positives in it. I told her the worst possible thing that could happen was that I would go to jail, and asked her what sort of positives she saw in that.

There was silence.

'Well,' she said eventually, 'you could become that comedian who's been to jail. That would be a good selling point, wouldn't it?'

I tried hypnotherapy. The hypnotherapist was a plump grey woman in her forties called Amanda, who had a kindly-aunt manner and operated out of a small, musty office up a little alley behind a dentist. The only other hypnotist I had seen was the 'Extraordinary Martin St James' in a plush auditorium at the North Sydney Leagues Club, so this was a bit of a comedown.

She explained that she would hypnotise me and then implant suggestions deep into my subconscious. I remembered Martin saying something similar, but hoped Amanda was going to do something more helpful than make me think I was a chicken every time someone said the word 'interval'.

'Now shut your eyes,' she said. I automatically obeyed. Maybe I was hypnotised already.

'Now, James, listen to me carefully,' said a big black man. My eyes jumped open but there was only Amanda smiling at me.

'Close your eyes and relax,' said the big black man's voice again. It was somehow coming out of Amanda's mouth. I tried not to smile, and the fact that I wanted to already made it $60 well spent.

'James, your eyes are heavy, you are going deeper and deeper,' said the voice. I tried to go with it.

'You are completely relaxed, and sliding deeper.'

I wanted to be hypnotised. I really did. It could help me.

'Your eyelids are heavy. You are going deeper.'

Yes, I was. Wasn't I?

'All your cares are drifting away as you go deeper and deeper. You are so deep that your conscious mind has let go and is floating and still you go deeper and deeper.'

Any minute now, I'm sure.

'Your breath is slow and steady and you are going deeper.'

No, actually I'm not.

'Deeper and deeper.'

Maybe it was my fault. I couldn't let go, I was incapable of relaxing. I was a remedial hypnotisee. The only thing going deeper and deeper was her voice.

'You are now in a deep hypnotic trance,' she said, which sounded very impressive, except that I wasn't.

I thought about letting her know that we had actually got a bit ahead of ourselves, but I didn't want to draw attention to her, or our, or my, failure. Poor thing, stuck in a leaky back room. To be honest, she probably lost me with the lack of props. Martin had had a big gold medallion that he waved about and that's the sort of thing I expected from a hypnotist. Without props I felt cheated.

She continued, telling my subconscious that it would let go of all anxiety, live in the present and embrace the possibilities of every moment. It sounded great.

When she'd finished I opened my eyes and looked dazedly around the room, trying to give the impression of being dis-orientated. I almost said 'where am I?' but thought that might be laying it on a bit thick.

After I shelled out, I tried to end on something positive. 'Thanks very much. That stuff about embracing the possibilities of every moment really made sense.'

Then I realised that if I had been in a deep hypnotic trance I wouldn't have known she'd said that. From the look she gave me I think she realised it too. I scuttled out.

eight

a ferry to rydalmere

What I should have done was spend a month catching ferries. It's hard to worry about anything on a ferry.

The plan was to catch one from Circular Quay up the harbour, past where it became a river, to Parramatta. To get the complete public transport experience we decided to first get the bus to Bondi Junction, then the train into the city.

People on buses and trains look as if they are trying to endure the trip, so that when it ends, if they have managed to survive, their lives can begin again. I've never seen anyone over the age of fifteen giggle on a bus or a train, unless they were drunk and irritating. The prepared bury their heads in a newspaper or book, while the rest either stare enviously at the prepared or memorise the map on the front wall of the carriage that shows how all the train stations connect. (They, curiously, are on both buses and trains.)

The good thing about the bus is that it is able to push into traffic. On buses the rear-view mirror is purely decorative. The driver may look in it to admire the view, but no matter what he sees behind him he's still going to pull out, and it's up to everyone else to get out of the way. And they do. The bad thing about the bus is all the stops. Just when you're about to press home the advantage that all the pushing-in has afforded you and really get going, there's another stop. They're way too close together. In most parts of Sydney people at different bus stops can talk to each other.

'It's good this one, you should come up here. There's this great whisky ad on the shelter. It's really artistic.'

'Nah, the bus'll get to this one first and I'll get a seat. You'll have to stand.'

Trains feel more modern. You go underground and get a ticket from a machine, then a disembodied female voice, which sounds as if its owner is wearing a very sensible beige suit, tells you that the next train on platform one is going to 'Cronulla. First stop Edgecliff. Then Kings Cross. Then all stations to Redfern,' etc. Twenty seconds later, it tells you again. Then again. And again. And so on. Great if you have Alzheimer's. Or if you like being told things over and over again.

You can watch telly on the platform too, although it's only ads, news, ads, weather and ads. Of course if you don't want to watch it you can just face the other way, and if you don't want to hear it, well, tough. It's on.

There's more room on a train, but from Bondi Junction to the city, less of a view. Unless you like tunnels. Actually, even if you do like tunnels it's not much of a view because, as you're in a tunnel, it's too dark to see the tunnel. There is, however, a good view of the entrance to and exit from the tunnel.

In every carriage there's at least one person who everyone else stares at. Bondi Junction is at the end of the Eastern Suburbs line, so when a train gets there and everyone gets off, all the seats are facing what was forwards, but on the way back will be backwards. There's always someone, usually a tourist, who gets on first and sits at what they think is the back of the carriage. Then everyone else gets on, flicks their seat across to face forwards on the way to town, and soon the carriage is full of front-facing passengers all staring at the poor person trapped on the only backward-facing seat. They either have to tough it out and stare right back, trying to give the impression that they prefer travelling backwards and being stared at, or accept the humiliation of acknowledging they've made a mistake and get up and swap the seat over. If they go for the second option, it is almost certain that they will be sitting on the one seat in the carriage that is broken and won't flick over and thus get stuck fruitlessly wrestling with it, which of course triples their embarrassment.

The train is efficient. You're in town before you know it and if you scavenge you can usually find a newspaper a commuter has previously absorbed and discarded. Everyone usually gets a seat, unless it's peak hour when only the lucky and the ruthless do. (I've always thought that those with something to read should get priority for seats because if they have to stand they miss out on more.)

But I feel incomplete at the end of a train trip, because there's no one to thank. We all just slink off to push into the escalator queue and deliver our tickets to a machine. On a bus there's that nice moment at the end when you thank the driver. Hell, he was only doing his job but he did it well. Didn't crash, at least. And you get to find out which of your fellow passengers are not as nice as you (the ones who don't say thank you).

We emerged into Martin Place, the centre of big end of town action. It's a long dark space 30 metres across that runs half a kilometre east–west up the city for five blocks. If it was meant as a break from buildings and streets then it's been successful, but it hasn't become anything more than that. It's a place people walk through, not to. It hasn't quite become anything more than that road-shaped bit in the middle of the city where there isn't actually a road.

Part of Martin Place's problem may be that, unlike its cousin Pitt Street Mall (are places and malls cousins? siblings? enemies?), which is flanked by places of commerce such as music, clothing, book and food shops, Martin Place is flanked by places that allow for the creation of infrastructure that facilitates the occurrence of commerce—like banks, law firms, merchant banks, insurance companies, investment banks, and other types of banks. Slightly less exciting. Unless you're a banker.

Even when they put on free lunchtime entertainment in the Martin Place amphitheatre (which, uniquely for an amphitheatre, doubles as an entrance to the train station) you get the feeling that the seats fill up mainly because, hey, what else are you going to do in your lunch hour while you eat your sandwich and try to forget about banking. There's only one road with seats in it and this is it.

Few linger in Martin Place, except backpackers and tourists who feel that, given it's where the GPO is, they should stay a few minutes as a sign of respect. Far more numerous when we arrived were the suited-up and briefcased, all hurrying as if they were late, or important, or both. Each, no doubt, had pressing concerns, important deadlines and phone calls, emails, faxes, pagers, text messages and even real people to respond to, but I wondered if anything would actually have gone wrong if I had produced a Pied Piper-style flute and led them all onto the ferry for a morning of skiving off.

It's important to be nice, but it's even more important to feel like you're important. Ten years earlier my corporate lawyer boss had rung me three days into his holiday to sort out all the problems that must have cropped up in his absence.

When I told him there weren't any he'd sounded kind of disappointed.

We headed down to Circular Quay past Macquarie Place, a far smaller, triangular-shaped public space that works, possibly because one side of the triangle is a pub from which alcohol is allowed to be bought and drunk outside. Sydney has never been as good as it should be at getting outside eating and drinking spaces right. Oxford Street in Darlinghurst/Paddington, King Street in Newtown, Campbell Parade on Bondi Beach and many more should have it down pat, but to our eternal shame, non-sunny Melbourne does the outdoor café infinitely better.

From Macquarie Place it's another couple of hundred metres to Circular Quay. As you approach the quay, beautiful harbour views should open up, but tragically they don't. The raised railway line that cuts Circular Quay off from the city is right up there with the Bondi Beach carpark in terms of architectural stuff-ups. It's an enormous barrier that removes the harbour from the city so that as you descend the hill toward the water you don't see water, you see concrete. It's not just a railway line—there's a road above it too, the Cahill Expressway, so the whole thing does facilitate the moving of lots of people who need to move, but the only reason there aren't continual complaints about it being an eyesore is that everyone has got used to it.

The upside is that once you pass under the railway it's as if you have been completely removed from the city. Expansive harbour views open up and the average walking pace decreases from just shy of Commonwealth Games qualifying (not Olympic Games qualifying, that would be exaggerating) to a leisurely meander. No one hurries by the water, or walks as if they think they're important.

There are always buskers at the Quay, and a cut above the normal standard, too. There must be an entrance exam. Rather than acoustic Neil Young and Nirvana, you get West Indian drums, puppet shows and good street theatre (not three words that often fit accurately together), the best example of which was a mimic who followed a metre behind his 'target', imitating exactly their walk and mannerisms until they noticed, at which point he would immediately turn on his heel and surf the wake of someone going back the other way. The highlight was when a young ocker bloke turned around, caught him and didn't like it, and the mimic showed he could do voices too.

'Whadayafuckin' doin?' Steps toward him.

'Whadayafuckin' doin?' Steps toward him.

'Don't get fuckin' smart, mate. Whadayafuckin' dooon?' Waves hands about.

'Don't get fuckin' smart, mate. Whadayafuckin' dooon?' Waves hands about.

'Oim fuckin' tellin' ya.' Jabs right index finger.

'Oim fuckin' tellin' ya.' Jabs right index finger.

It was only when the bloke pulled back his fist that the busker took off on someone else's tail, drawing a huge round of applause from all around except the potential puncher, who looked as if he wanted to deck us all, then gave us the finger and took off.

Ferries to Parramatta only go once an hour but we'd timed our run to perfection. Or at least we thought we had.

'It's been cancelled,' said the bloke behind the glass when I tried to buy tickets.

I waited for him to tell me why. He didn't.

'Why?' I asked.

'Dunno, mate.'

'Really?'

'Just happens sometimes.'

One difference between ferries and trains is that if the train you wanted to catch, say the 4.51 p.m. to Cronulla, was cancelled you wouldn't just catch the next one, the 4.54 p.m. to Strathfield instead, because you thought you might enjoy the trip.

That's what we did with the ferry, though. We had a choice of two: to Rydalmere or Cremorne. Neither of us knew anything about Rydalmere and it was also up the river, the last stop before Parramatta. Perfect.

Another difference between ferries and other methods of public transport is that ferries have their names proudly displayed on the side. Ours was *Marjorie Jackson*, after the sprinter (or the ferry-namers just thought it was a nice name), and we took a seat outside at the front with the tourists while a group of old people on a day trip took the inside.

We started off by reversing away from the jetty, which felt strange. Reversing is so car-like, as was the three-point turn *Marjorie* did to get going toward the bridge.

'Excuse me, do you know what there is to do at Rydalmere?' said the fiftyish man next to me in a thick German accent.

'I've got no idea, I'm sorry,' I admitted. 'You've come a long way.'

'Yes, I am from Adelaide,' he replied, deadpan. 'But 20 years ago, I lived in Rydalmere.'

'You lived in Rydalmere?'

'Yes.'

'And you don't know what there is to do in Rydalmere?'

'No.'

'Right.'

Perhaps we should have picked Cremorne.

Ferries are God's buses. A road train or track can't compare with the sea. You suck in the salty air, feel the breeze and the spray and worry about whether you are being a bad parent by exposing your child to winds that could give her a nasty chill that might develop into pneumonia.

You can't overrate the sea. Yes, it's made of the same stuff that comes out of the tap but when it's all around I can't help but feel better about everything. It's a mood booster. If you're feeling okay, the sea will up it to good, good on land will be boosted to great on the water, and great will become ecstatic. Even suicidal on land becomes merely very depressed at sea.

There was a bit of wind, but the water was calm, so no one nearly fell overboard. Unlike last time.

Six months earlier we had been staying at Lucy's parents' house on the Central Coast and had discovered that a ferry ran from Ettalong, just down the road, across Broken Bay to Palm Beach. While the idea of leaving Sydney for a holiday and then taking a day trip back to Sydney was weird, we convinced ourselves that Palm Beach was only technically Sydney. Its essence was posh coastal town.

Bibi was six months old and before we boarded we swaddled her up so she looked like a blanket with a face. On board, downstairs was closed in and full of rows of pleasant seats protected from the elements by closed windows. Not for us—we wanted the full experience so we headed upstairs into the open.

We picked seats at the front and admired the big view south of Broken Bay. Lion Island sat in the middle with the Hawkesbury River heading inland to its right, and the ocean opening out to its left. Past it was Barrenjoey Head and beyond it Pittwater and Palm Beach.

'Why would you sit inside and miss out on this?' I said.

As we set off the conductor popped his head up and addressed us and the only other passengers upstairs, a twentyish couple in either love or lust.

'You might want to come downstairs. It can get a bit choppy up here.'

I gave him a knowing smile. 'We'll be right, thanks.'

I knew boats.

The sea was glass and the slight rocking motion moved Bibi to pleasured squeals. We were pointing and laughing and looking. Even the couple behind us had stopped feeling each other up for a few seconds to admire the view.

Then we rounded the heads into Broken Bay. Instantly we were on one of those fun-park rides you pay $10 to get on and then within a minute would pay $50 to get off. We were pitching and yawing and other nautical-terming and someone hiding just over the side of the ferry was throwing buckets of water at us. Bibi kept squealing but the tone and meaning had changed. She had been squealing 'fun', now it was 'not fun, anti-fun, bad fun, scared, scared, help'.

I looked over my shoulder to see how the lovers were coping. The gutless wonders had disappeared, hopefully downstairs and not overboard. We wanted to be downstairs as well, but getting there was a problem. We were at the front of the boat, the stairs were at the back. The floor was wet and slippery, the boat was pitching, we had two bags and Bibi was a baby.

'Forget the bags,' I yelled, 'you grab Bibi and I'll grab you.'

Lucy wrapped both arms around Bibi, and I grabbed Lucy around the waist with one hand and steadied myself by grabbing a chair with the other. Then we all tried to stand up. The deck pitched and we crashed back down again. We tried again and got to our feet. Lucy would have been over in a second if I hadn't been holding her, and I would have too if I hadn't been holding a seat with my other hand. The three of us, Bibi, held by Mummy, held by Daddy, slowly inched and staggered our way back to the stairs. Eventually we got there, drenched and shaken.

At the bottom of the stairs the boat seemed calm, or nearly

so, but a level up the effect of any roll was double what it was at sea level.

'The bags,' I said. 'I'll go back and get them.'

Upstairs the pitching and yawing and other nautical-terming seemed to have gotten worse. I had to crawl back along the aisle on all fours, then put both shoulder straps in my teeth and crawl back, dragging the bags backwards to the stairs. Thank goodness I was alone; I looked ridiculous. Back downstairs I tried to compose and dry myself before walking with as much dignity as I could to where Lucy and Bibi were sitting.

It was only when we were pulling into Palm Beach wharf that I noticed the screen, twice television-size, next to the driver. It showed, from a fixed camera, the entire upper deck; my attempts at regaining dignity had been fruitless. The whole bottom level had seen me staggering, then crawling, up top, and because the camera was fixed and confined its view to the deck, rather than including the sea, you couldn't actually see how violently the top deck was rocking. They'd all seen me crawling and falling, and dragging two bags in my teeth, along a seemingly placid deck.

Our harbour ferry was luckily just one storey high and there was no open ocean or video camera. We chugged under the Harbour Bridge heading west to Parramatta. No, west to Rydalmere.

You can divide Sydney north–south or east–west, and the harbour is a perfect spot to do it from. (You can also divide Sydney into 'near the water' and 'not near the water', but the harbour isn't a perfect place to do that from because everything you can see from it is near the water, except for the water, which is the water.)

Obvious difference number one: west of the Harbour Bridge there are houses on the north side and apartments on the south side—dozens of new, same-looking blocks, with owners all holding their breath and hoping the property bubble doesn't burst. (Bad luck—it has.) At Breakfast Point, on the south side opposite Gladesville, was a 3-kilometre stretch of dirt that was either a desert theme park or about to become the king of all apartment blocks. As we got further up the river I expected things to spread out a bit, but the apartments on the south side continued to squeeze tight, crammed together in places that, quite frankly, didn't look worth cramming together for. I wondered how they advertised them—'All the disadvantages of cramped inner-city living without the convenience of actually being near anywhere' perhaps.

It just shows the power of water. People will sacrifice a lot to be able to see it out their window.

Northside, everyone has their own garden. Some even have their own beach. Not a Manly-style beach, mind—most are only a 20-metre bit of sand hiding between two shabby jetties that you can't jump into the water from because of the sharks and pollution—but nonetheless a beach. It would be perfect for those who like boating or have very low expectations of beaches, or who just like being able to drop into a conversation, 'when I was down at our beach this morning'.

We passed the Abbotsford 12-Foot Flying Squadron. Funny place for an airport; you'd think near the water they'd have a sailing club.

The ferry goes slowly enough to allow a good thorough look, but fast enough that it doesn't get boring, and more or less alternates between stops northside then southside, so you get to see a bit of everything. I saw a rich man in his garden on the north side, and a poorer one in his communal outside apartment space on the south. Few people got on or off on the north side (they don't need public transport) while the southside stops were busier.

At Cabarita the group of oldies sitting inside got off. Had

they had their day trip or was it just beginning? Presumably they had come from Cabarita on an adventure to the city, rather than the other way round. The name Cabarita, by the way, derives from an Aboriginal word thought to mean 'by the water', which is an immaculately accurate, if not a terribly imaginative or unique description.

Around Gladesville, east–west differences become apparent. The houses on the north side get smaller and then are gradually replaced by blocks of flats. On the south side apartment complexes get less shiny, bright and expensive looking.

By the way, 'flat' and 'apartment' are not interchangeable terms. 'Apartment' is a new property-boom term that has been appropriated from America by developers and real estate agents who don't think the term 'flat' sounds glamorous enough to justify the amount of money they want people to pay. 'Flats' are things that were there before the late-nineties property boom. Apartments are new. Flats are usually brown or brick coloured, while apartments have been rendered and then desperately painted something bright that shouts 'I'M NEW' (usually pink, sky blue, a trendy brown subtly distinct from old flat brown, or something vaguely metallic), so they can be desperately sold at 'I'M NEW' prices. As the property boom falters, and the owners panic, the paint gets brighter.

By north-side Meadowbank, just 6 kilometres west of rich Hunters Hill, we were in the western suburbs. No more mansions, no more private beaches, just flats and modest houses. They, in turn, soon gave way on the north side to marshes and swamps overhung with mangroves. These are a new addition, apparently, since European arrival, so I hope whatever thrives on mangroves is grateful.

On the south side we docked at Homebush Bay. Homebush Bay is, of course, where the Olympics were held and, judging from the area's development since then, that is all Homebush will ever be remembered for. Unless one day it hosts the Olympics again.

I would love to tell you that since the Olympics, Homebush Bay has gone from strength to strength and is now a thriving and cosmopolitan business centre, residential area and sports training facility. But it's not. It's a ghost town or, more accurately, since ghost towns were once real towns and Homebush never was, a ghost collection of stadiums and training facilities. It's a wonderful place to be alone. Walking around, you see more stadiums than people. It would be the perfect place for a Buddhist retreat.

A couple of lonely hotels eke out a living from badly advised and no doubt (once they see where they are stuck), really pissed-off tourists and, yes, they have conferences and sporting events and athletes probably train there, but if you walk around Homebush Bay you will feel as if you are walking around a school in the middle of the Christmas holidays. There's nothing to see except the outsides of big, functional, grey buildings.

Even the leisure and tourism link website seems to acknowledge it's all over for Homebush. They advertise tours of the big stadium, but when I looked the price and other information on the website hadn't been updated for nearly three years, since February 2001. Even then it was pricey to have a look; $26 for adults, half that for kiddies and $19.50 for pensioners. And that's when there isn't even anything on.

As we docked at Homebush Bay, four German tourists, a separate group from the Rydalmere Adelaidean German, strapped their backpacks on.

'Don't do it,' I felt like shouting, 'it's a trap.' But politeness and good manners held me back, and I let them walk the gangplank to their doom, or at least bore*doom*. As the ferry pressed on I felt a pang of guilt as their jaunty gait carried them closer and closer, they thought, to where the action was. What they didn't know was that the ferry they just got off is the closest Homebush Bay ever gets to action.

Homebush was the last sign of civilisation, if you can call it that. The harbour had narrowed to a river about 40 metres wide with dense swampy mangroves and bush closing in on it on both sides.

'It's like something out of *The African Queen*,' said Lucy.

'Except they didn't have smokestacks coming out of the tops of the trees.' There were about four of them, politely reminding us that, no, we weren't in deepest, darkest Africa, and that heavy industry was just a hundred or so metres away. You could smell it, too. Burning factory stuff.

I was thinking of a different movie: *Apocalypse Now*. We were going up the river, not to kill Colonel Kurtz, but on a mission that might be even harder to accomplish—to find something to do at Rydalmere. I love the smell of burning factory stuff in the morning.

All right, it had just gone midday, but it was close enough.

Around another bend the mangroves opened to reveal a dock packed with hundreds of truck-sized containers fresh from a ship. What did they contain? Kettles, teddy bears, shoes, exercise bikes?

Then our destination. We docked on the north side of the river at Rydalmere. There were only us and the Adelaide German left. He sighed, picked up his backpack and walked off to search for his past. I picked up Bibi and we walked after him.

Rydalmere is one of the few suburbs that hasn't privatised its foreshore. Rather than houses or apartments and flats coming right to the river, there is a 40-metre wide stretch of parkland running along the water. On the other side of the park are houses, although upriver they become factories. North of the jetty is industrial Rydalmere, south of it residential Rydalmere.

We decided to strike out upriver—west—first, but after a hundred metres came to a fence surrounding a factory. 'Beware of snakes,' said a sign behind the wire. Normally when you have to beware of snakes the consolation is that you are somewhere in nature, not next to a factory. It seemed a bit unfair, the worst of both worlds.

There was a narrow pedestrian bridge attached to a pipeline that led over to the south side of the river. As we climbed the stairs, three men in factory grey hurried past us, going the other way. The view at the top was of a huge factory yard full of more shipping containers being moved about by forklifts. Another grey-dressed man walked vigorously past, looking anxiously ahead as if trying to catch the first three. We turned around and followed him back.

As we walked back to the jetty the three men passed us again, now heading back to the bridge. The same distance behind them was the fourth man, still looking as if he was trying to catch up. What was going on? A desperate industrial drama that could end in treachery and violence, or a lunchtime exercise kick?

We headed downriver, then cut inland. We'd seen the river, now for residential Rydalmere. What lurked within a suburb that I had, in eighteen years in Sydney, never once thought about, except when I had first heard its name and thought, *And I thought Ryde had a strange name.*

Rydalmere is an average suburb full of average houses. There is plenty of room and very little to do. It offers typical suburban life. You do your living elsewhere, then come home and hide from the world.

Some of the houses have nice gardens. Some don't. Some are new and some are old and some have been knocked down to build apartment blocks to fit more people in. We saw virtually no one, but it was a Thursday morning and people clearly had more important things to do than wander the streets looking for action. And if you were going to wander the streets looking for action, you wouldn't do it in Rydalmere. You'd pick somewhere more exciting, like Homebush.

It's very quiet. It's peaceful, and may well be a nice place to come home to, but if you were unemployed or retired or even worked from home, I imagine it could get very lonely.

The occasional house was special. One had a fake rock wall, a plaster of Paris cliff-face stuck on the front of the house. Why would you do that to a house? For rock-climbing practice? But if you tried to climb it, it would break. Another had a mini wishing-well in the front garden. A cunning plan to lure coins from passers-by? Fatal flaw: there were no passers-by. We wandered about, found a swing for Bibi and then made our way back to the ferry.

If we had found something at Rydalmere that was fascinating, or even quite interesting, it would have beautifully exemplified the point that if you look hard enough, and if you have the right attitude, you can find fun and excitement anywhere. That's what we hoped we'd discover, that the most important thing when we went to a particular place wasn't whether there were lovely views or interesting sights, but our attitude. But in Rydalmere we came up empty.

As we headed back to the jetty an unkempt front garden reminded me of the one I used to pretend to be a gardener in as community service at school. We had a choice of cadets, scouts or gardening for an old person, and I'd love to say I wanted to help others much more than I wanted to learn how to hold a gun or discover the joys of knot-tying, but the real reason I picked community service was that it was a known soft option.

Mrs Anderson was an 83-year-old widow who kept offering to pay me for my work, not because it was good but because she didn't want to be a charity case. Every Sunday morning I'd visit her and prune and weed as directed. Sort of. My heart wasn't in it, and she soon noticed. After my fifth Sunday she came out at the end of the hour, had a look around then said she thought it would be better if I didn't come any more.

'Why?'

'Because you don't do a proper job. You don't care.'

The obvious truth of what she was saying didn't prevent me from feeling outraged. I tried to persuade her that my attitude was fine, it was just that I was hopelessly incompetent, but she was adamant. And correct. I didn't care. I had been doing some very poor gardening. As I rode my bike home I felt slightly guilty. And relieved that I didn't have to go back. The next day I just felt relieved.

Rydalmere was the first place we'd been to that we had written off. As we got back on the ferry, once again I felt slightly guilty, but by the time we arrived back at Circular Quay I didn't feel guilty anymore. I just felt relieved that I didn't have to go back.

The trip back was, as it always is, not quite as good as the trip there, but because we were on a ferry it was still good. The Germans didn't rejoin us at Homebush which worried me. Either the stadium suburb's turbo-charged boredom had sapped their will and they were staring stupor-like at a velodrome, unable to summon the will to move, or perhaps, even more frighteningly, they had found Homebush interesting. I'm no fan of cultural stereotypes but if they had found it interesting, then surely the one about Germans being very dull had just been reinforced.

We made one mistake on the return trip. We bought the paper. And because we had it, I read it, and suddenly I didn't feel like we were on holiday any more, looking out at whatever caught the eye, but as if we were commuting, using the time we needed to spend getting from A to B as efficiently as possible by sucking in all the news we could. It was a little thing, but it made a big difference.

My final word on ferries is this: catch one soon. I don't care where. Please, you'll enjoy it. Some people want to change the world. I just want to persuade you to catch a ferry to somewhere you don't necessarily need to go. Just for the trip.

nine

chemicals

Unlike Ivan who was always fussing about at number eighteen, Alan and Sally on the other side had the good sense to stay out of the way of their builders. The labourer there was a big Eastern European man with curly black hair and a perpetually cheerful face.

'How old you think I am?' he asked me one morning as he was wheelbarrowing loads of dirt up a steeply-angled plank into a skip.

I hate being asked that. You always have to estimate, then subtract ten years so as not to offend. Unless the asker is under twenty-five-ish, in which case you have to add on two years so as not to offend.

'Um . . . gee (sixty minus ten equals), fifty?'

'Sixty-two,' he said proudly, the pride I assumed coming from the fact that he thought he looked younger than he was, rather than from the fact that, nearing the end of his working life, he was still a builder's labourer.

'Gosh.'

'Sixty-two.'

'Gee.'

'Ya. Sixty-two.' He kept looking expectantly at me, as if I was supposed to show how amazed I was at his youthfulness by doing something more dramatic, like fainting.

'There you go, hey,' I said.

'Sixty-two. How old you are?'

'Thirty-seven.'

'Really!'

'Yeah.'

'You look older. A lot older.'

'Ah,' I said, which was far more polite than saying what I wanted to say. I only said that under my breath after I went inside.

At number twenty-two they seemed to be doing almost all of their work on the common wall. They spent entire days bashing, belting and drilling into it, as if it had some vital information about where the gold was hidden and wouldn't talk. What had the wall done to them? Before Dorothy died I had been inside her house and seen number twenty-two's side of the wall and it had seemed to me to be a fine looking wall, a wall that other walls around the world could look up to and aspire to be like. There were no holes in it. It wasn't falling apart. It wasn't a spy. It may have needed a coat of paint but torturing it wasn't going to achieve anything. Whenever they smashed at it my eyes would leap around the room looking for the builders, because the noise was so loud in our living room that surely they had to be inside our house doing it from this side. Then I'd go and grab Bibi because she would have started crying.

As they continued to bash away at the wall, and the wall continued bravely refusing to talk, cracks started to appear on our side of the wall near the roof, and the paint started to come off.

I first noticed it when I was making a cup of tea and a line of fine white powder trickled into it from above. I looked up and saw the roof flaking. I stared at the wall, through it to the noise and the builders, and shouted.

'I DON'T FUCKING TAKE FUCKING SUGAR.'

Then I felt embarrassed and hoped they hadn't heard me.

The hypnotherapy, needless to say, didn't work. Eventually I got around to wondering, since I was incredibly anxious almost all of the time, whether I might have an anxiety disorder. In early 1997, six months after I started to get anxious, I saw a doctor and got a referral to see a psychiatrist, to try to find out if I did.

I paced nervously up and down the street outside. To walk through the door into the office of a psychiatrist was to admit that I had a mental health problem. I didn't have to admit that to see a hypnotherapist. I had friends who had seen hypnotherapists to help them give up smoking or to forget about a girlfriend who didn't love them anymore. But I didn't know anyone who said they had a mental health problem.

Things felt out of control. I was scared of not being able to control my continual worrying, which sounded to me like a mental health problem. So I went in.

Eventually I was shown into the doctor's room. He instantly impressed me as being very, very smart. That was good. I answered all sorts of questions about my habits and thought patterns: did I do this? did I worry about that? I tried to answer as fully as I could, but in retrospect I realise that I slanted my answers to give the impression that my anxiety was a function of my job, when in reality it was a function of my mind.

The doctor eventually told me he didn't think I had classic anxiety disorder. My problem was very specifically focused and

I didn't have the accompanying symptoms and behaviors usually associated with an anxiety disorder.

'Really?' I said, trying to sound calm. But I was devastated. If only I had run around the house continually re-checking that the windows were locked, and scrubbing already spotless cereal bowls, maybe I would have been in.

'I do, however, think that you could benefit from anti-depressants.'

WHAT!

So far I had managed to get through by clinging to the idea that I was a normal chap behaving very bravely in difficult circumstances. The idea that I might have an anxiety disorder was acceptable—barely—because an anxiety disorder was some-thing unpleasant but eccentric, something that could be worked on and fixed, like a bad backhand, via exercises designed specif-ically to strengthen the mind.

When someone told me they had an anxiety disorder my eyebrows would go up, and then I'd look back at them and say, 'Gosh. What's that?' But if they told me they were on anti-depressants I'd look at the ground and wouldn't quite know what to say.

Not that anyone would tell you. Depression carried a big stigma that I didn't want to go near.

'But they're chemicals,' I said.

The doctor laughed. They probably don't teach doctors to respond to questions from anxious and uncertain patients that way in medical school, but it worked. I like laughter, and I'd been missing it.

'What do you think everything you eat is made of?' he said. 'Your lunch is chemicals.'

He persuaded me to give them a go. I was feeling so rundown and raw by this time it wasn't hard. He sent me back to the GP, who sent me to the chemist. The anti-depressants helped a bit, I think, although it's impossible to know. They certainly didn't make my anxiety go away. That remained with me almost constantly, but the pills may have reduced its effect from really, really bad to really bad. And once I was taking them, I was too scared to stop taking them in case their absence made things worse.

Being on anti-depressants changed my view of the world. Not the drugs themselves. I didn't notice any real effect on my thinking, and neither did Lucy, who I asked to assess whether I was changing in any way. I had visions of the drugs doing what they did in *One Flew Over the Cuckoo's Nest*, draining my brain of power and taking the edge off my thinking, but that didn't happen. In fact, while I was on them I was as productive as I had ever been in my life. I wrote and performed a one-hour, one-man comedy show, did a lot of stand-up, worked as a lawyer three days a week, wrote five days a week for a breakfast radio show and did bits and pieces of TV and radio. Ironically, in my time of chronic anxiety when nothing was funny, my comedy career took off.

It wasn't what the drugs did, it was the fact of being on them that changed my view of the world. The world had been something I had been pretty confident about up until September 1996. Since I had started to try and take control of what I was doing five years earlier things had turned out pretty well. Whereas most people I knew complained about their one job, I had two I enjoyed. Being a legal aid criminal lawyer had great cred in a way that being a corporate lawyer didn't; I loved the way people's reaction would turn 180 degrees after their second question.

'What do you do?'

'I'm a lawyer.'

'Oh (how boring), what sort?'

'Criminal.'

'Really? (suddenly interested).'

Add on the cred provided by stand-up comedy and I, who had always found the approval of others very important (why else would you do stand-up comedy?), was perceived as a pretty interesting guy. I also had the additional confidence that comes with being in a good, secure relationship. All up, prior to September 1996 things were tickety-boo. After years of not really being sure why I was here, I was beginning to feel the world was my oyster.

I didn't feel like that when I was on anti-depressants. The confidence I had was undermined by the fact that I knew I needed medication to look the world in the eye; that I couldn't do it on my own. Ironically, one of the things that made me depressed was the very fact that I was on anti-depressants.

Eventually the anxiety ended. It just sort of faded away. There was no miracle cure, no moment of enlightenment or realisation, but one day I felt secure enough to start tentatively reducing my medication. A couple of months later, the idea that I had been on anti-depressants at all seemed ridiculous. I was back to normal—completely. While the anxiety I had experienced had been huge and horrible, I hadn't been changed by it. It was as if I'd had a cold and now it was gone. I wasn't damaged by what had happened, I wasn't wiser because of it, I didn't appreciate the everyday pleasures of life any more or less as a result, it was just over.

ten

loudspeakers in paradise

Ivan was hands-on at his new house. Literally. He didn't just appear to watch and fuss and make unhelpful suggestions and try to hurry the builders up, like most owners. Ivan came to the site to work. Every day. There's a hierarchy on building sites. It varies a bit around the top and middle but the labourers are always at the bottom. They are those without a trade, who haven't done an apprenticeship, whose job it is to carry and dig. The carpenters, plumbers, electricians and tilers do their specialty bits, but the beating heart of a building site is the worker bees, the labourers. They do the hardest work and get paid the least and hence their status is the lowest. When Ivan came to work he did not come with the status of an owner. He did not come with the status of a labourer. He came in at a new level never before seen on a building site—below the labourers.

Ivan wanted to learn how to build a house and this was how he was going to do it. He would start, not at the bottom but one step below the bottom, and he would do all the jobs that the labourers, who got all the shitty jobs, found the most shitty and wanted to off-load. I had to admire his commitment.

The labourers had never had anyone to order around before, much less the guy who was paying their wages, and at first they found it hard.

'Joe. Can you dig those footings out?'

'Yeah. Fuckin', um . . . Ivan . . . would you, . . . fuckin' . . . um . . . if you like you can help me dig these footings out a bit. Would that be all right?'

And Ivan would look like he'd just been asked if he'd like some free gold. He'd dive in. Keen as. Awkward as, too (although no more than I would have been), but he was as enthusiastic as a property developer after a playground up for re-zoning. The shittier the job the more eagerly Ivan responded. It seemed that for him, after digging away a hill with a milk crate, anything was a step up. He never said no. He never complained. He would emerge at the end of the day with beard covered in dust, concrete through his hair, clothes filthy, cuts on his elbows, his big glasses hanging crooked and covered in smudged mud so that he had to peer over them to see, the smallest by 15 kilos and the oldest by twenty years, looking near death, but also proud. He was building his big house himself. The bigger it got, the prouder he looked.

Soon the labourers got used to ordering Ivan around. They had worked out he never said no and never complained, and that no matter what they asked him to do, he never pulled rank. They realised they didn't have to treat him like an owner. When he arrived in the morning they started to greet him with a chorus of fake Russian accents.

'Ivan!'

'Ivan!'

'Ivan!'

Their attitude towards him was basically one of acceptance, but they knew he wasn't really one of them. They did this work because they had to. For Ivan, it was just his new hobby.

They also worked out that Ivan was not exactly Nureyev with workboots. No wonder, he'd never done it before. But the deferential tone that had initially been used to address him slowly disappeared, as did the question mark at the end of their invitations to work. The 'fuckin's', always present somewhere in any next-door labourer sentence, changed in tone from friendly to businesslike.

'Ivan, dig out those fuckin' footings, okay.'

'No, Ivan. Deeper. Fuck. And squared off at the end.'

'Ivan, get the electric paint stripper and strip all the paint of that outside wall. Fuck.'

'Ivan. You have to go quicker. The fuckin' renderers are coming fuckin' tomorrow.'

'Watch it, Ivan! Fuck. You can't put beams there! One could slip off and scone someone! Jesus!'

'Fuck! Ivan!'

But he kept coming back for more. He was determination. Whatever work he was doing, carrying or paint-stripping or digging, he had the same look on his face, the one I'd first seen when he was milk-crating away the hill, the one that suggested that while what he was doing was not pleasant, he was damn well going to keep on until it was done. But I don't think that meant he hated what he was doing. I think that's just how he looked. Even when they all had a beer after work he looked like that.

At the end of each day, however, his look seemed to fractionally subside into something resembling satisfaction. It was the look of a kid who is finally allowed to join the cricket game.

Status, in Sydney, is not just about where you live. But it is mostly about where you live. The most important indicators of status, of the extent to which it appears from the outside that you have made it in Sydney, are, in descending order of importance:

1. Where you live.
Palm Beach is best (but only if it's a weekend retreat) followed by east on the coast, east slightly inland, then the North Shore. After that, generally the further away a suburb is from the city and the beach the less status living there has, subject to the fact that being near any naturally occurring body of water (except a gutter stream after a storm) significantly ups status. There are, however, some rogue suburbs that break all the rules. For example, Strathfield, the Vaucluse of the west, is not near the beach, the city or water and yet if you say you live there people will think you've made it (unless you're under 30, in which case they'll think you're old before your time).

Beach suburbs are, of course, high status and follow a rule. The status attached to Sydney's southern beach suburbs increases the nearer you are to Bronte Beach. On the north side, the gradual decline in status north from Manly begins to reverse around Narrabeen. North of Narrabeen status rises steeply again through Bilgola to Avalon and Whale Beach until it peaks at Palm Beach.

Having a water view attracts huge points. But water views are so ridiculously rare and expensive in Sydney that it is enough to have a view of a house that has a water view because then you can say, 'You can't quite see the water from here, but see that house over there. They can see it . . . so yeah, we're pretty close.'

It's not just about the area you live in; the name of the suburb is important, too. Potts Point and Kings Cross are right next to each other just east of the city, but while Potts Point has high status, Kings Cross doesn't (unless you're a junkie, in which case it's close to everything, that is, supply and places to shoot up).

Also in the east, Paddington and Woollahra are adjacent, but if you had two identical houses 10 metres apart, one either side of the dividing line, the Woollahra one would be worth substantially more.

What the name of a suburb says about that suburb can increase desirability to the uninitiated. Eastwood sounds like a genteel, forested glen in the eastern suburbs. In fact, it's in the north-west and is nowhere near a forest. Add 'heights' to anywhere—for example, next to and above Revesby is Revesby Heights—and it creates the impression of status, as if the residents live in grand castles, and watch protectively over their minions in mere Revesby from the turrets.

The namers of some Sydney suburbs obviously caught onto the fact that giving a suburb a name that suggests height elevates its social status and so some suburbs have dared to be 'somewhere heights' without there actually being a 'somewhere'.

They are:

Dover Heights (no Dover)

Elanora Heights (no Elanora)

Killarney Heights (ditto)

Lucas Heights (ditto)

Wheeler Heights (ditto)

Canley Heights (no Canley, although there is a romantic sounding Canley Vale)

Emu Heights (no Emu, although there is Emu Plains)

Georges Heights (no Georges, but there is a Georges Hall).

I'm not saying that Dover Heights isn't high. It is, but the name does suggest it's the high bit of the Dover area, when in actual fact it *is* the Dover area.

My favourite suburb name is the mystery, the enigma, the paradox that is Valley Heights. Surely it can't be both. If it's a valley, it's got to be surrounded by higher bits, and if it's surrounded higher bits, how can it call itself 'heights'? And what are they going to call the surrounding higher bits when people get around to building houses on them? Valley Heights Heights? Valley Heights is just west of Penrith and the Emus and no, there is no suburb called Valley. Or Mountain Lows.

Other descriptions that have been added to plain Sydney suburb names to make them sound better are: Hill (Bass Hill), Hills (Baulkham Hills), Vale, Gardens, Point, Bay, Park, Plateau, Downs and Fields. They all sound rural and rustic but don't be fooled. Most aren't. They may have been when they were named but they're not any more.

Finally, the status of some suburbs is upped by having a fully or partially French name. Two examples are Sans Souci, meaning 'without care', and Brighton-le-Sands, meaning 'Brighton the Sands'.

2. Owning or renting.
The next indicator of the extent to which you have made it in Sydney is whether you own or rent. Renting has negative status unless it's of a ridiculously expensive inner-city penthouse.

3. Mortgage.
If you own, there is the size of your mortgage to take into account. Traditionally, the smaller the mortgage the greater the status. Now, however, the property fetish has made debt trendy. Huge debt has huge status. Never let slip you have a mortgage under $200,000. People will think you're gutless. For men, mortgage size is the new penis size. Size is everything.

4. The sort of house.
What sort of house you live in is the next indicator of making it. In ascending order of status: under a bridge, flat, apartment, semi, free-standing house, mansion hidden behind the high walls of a guarded compound.

5. What condition your dwelling is in.
What sort of bridge do you live under and do you have plans to do it up? In ascending order of status, is your home:
- unrenovated/original/shitty
- being renovated
- renovated
- renovated once but about to be renovated again just because you have too much money and you can
- built from scratch after demolishing the old house
- built from scratch after demolishing the old house and about to be renovated again just because you have too much money and you can.

6. What you earn.

7. What you do.
(Some societies believe what you do is more important than what you earn and reverse 6 and 7. Weird, huh?)

8. Where you have holidays.
Overseas has high status, but not as high as 'at the farm' or 'at the shack'. Note: a beach house can only be called a shack if it isn't one. Shacks are fully done up, luxurious second homes at the beach. If it really is a shack, it should be called 'the beach house'.

9–114. Lots of other things.

115. How happy you are.

All of which brings me to La Perouse. A La Perouse address doesn't carry with it nearly as much status as it deserves. In other words, it's better than it's perceived to be. It's a hidden treasure. The French name isn't pretentious, by the way, it was named after someone, La Perouse, to be precise, whose two ships landed at Botany Bay in 1788 just five days after the First Fleet arrived. La Perouse had spent three years sailing from France around the bottom of South America to Alaska, Hawaii, Japan and then Australia. Next stop was to be the Solomon Islands but both his ships sank on the way. So he deserves at least a suburb named after him.

His suburb is at Botany Bay, in the same position relative to the bay as Manly is to the harbour, forming the northern headland that separates the bay from the ocean. It's a peninsula made up largely of beach and bush, and almost no houses, which is probably why it hasn't got the attention it deserves. If you can't buy it, most people couldn't give a stuff how pretty it is.

No one has yet realised La Perouse is the south side's Palm Beach (it's a lot closer to the city than Palm Beach: twenty minutes' drive compared to an hour) and the few who do live there have the extent to which they have made it severely underestimated. Maybe the fact you have to drive past Sydney's biggest jail, Long Bay, to get there interferes with the atmosphere a tad, but hell, those walls look big and sturdy to me. There is also the fact that unlike Palm Beach, which is surrounded by pristine water—ocean on one side and Pittwater on the other—La Perouse opens onto Botany Bay, a working port with an airport jutting into it. So it has a slightly less romantic image than that of the Northern beaches.

But don't be fooled. Between the jail, the port and the airport lies a hidden jewel. The only clue is the name: La

Perouse. French. Therefore exotic, romantic and sophisticated sounding. Yes, Palm Beach is a good name but ultimately it's functional. It tells you there's a beach, and that there are palms (presumably of the tree variety—you'd be a bit disappointed if it just meant there are lots of people there showing the fronts of their hands). But La Perouse suggests mystery, and once you know the bloke was an explorer, then it's even more intriguing.

Anyway, that's what we thought. Our expectations were high. Or at least mine and Lucy's were. Bibi was asleep in the back.

We drove south along Anzac Parade and soon it had left traffic lights behind and taken us all the way to the shores of Botany Bay. We parked, got out, turned left and descended twenty steps to a beautiful beach you could film scenes for the next remake of *Robinson Crusoe* on. There was no evidence we were in a city. We might have been 100 miles from the nearest shop. The beach is 150 metres long and faces south to Cronulla. At the far end—east—sand gave way to rocks gave way to bush, and we could see the coast curving away southeast, with bush rising behind it. A track led inland claiming it led to Henry's Head, 1.5 kilometres. We followed it and once again the bush wove its magic. The fight Lucy and I had had in the car over a big fat phone bill was forgotten. Trees closed in around us, taking the edge off the sun's heat, and lizards flickered at the edges of the track. Bibi was happy in the backpack and the gradually ascending slope promised a view at the top.

Then:

'WILL MR ANDREWS, MR WILLIAMS AND PARTY PLEASE MAKE THEIR WAY TO THE FIRST TEE. AT 10.35 MR LOOSEMORE'S PARTY WILL

BE ABLE TO TEE OFF. AT 10.40 THE FIRST TEE WILL BE AVAILABLE FOR MR MATTHEWS AND HIS PARTY.'

The voice boomed and the lizards ran away. It sounded close and yet all we could see was bush. Soon we came to the top of a rise and away to our left was a big cleared space partially filled with golf course and clubhouse. While national park skirts around the shoreline, the New South Wales Golf Club occupies most of the rest of the La Perouse peninsula, except for the bits occupied by a pistol range, another golf course, St Michaels, and yet another golf course, The Coast. And as you head up the coast past the golf course, the pistol range and the golf courses, further north is another golf course and a rifle range. All up, an almost continuous 10-kilometre stretch of prime coastal land from Botany Bay to Maroubra, worth tens, maybe hundreds, of millions of dollars, all given over to shooting and hitting. What's going on?

I suppose you could argue that if the land was all national park and picnic grounds, only bushwalkers and picnickers could use it, and the minority groups of golfers and shooters have just as much right to some land for their hobbies as the minority groups of bushwalkers and picnickers. That, however, would ignore the fact that a lot more people picnic and bushwalk than shoot and hit. And it would ignore the fact that a lot more people *should* bushwalk and picnic than shoot and hit. Trying to get something small to arrive accurately somewhere else, as both golf and shooting do, is not inherently useful. In fact, getting good at shooting can be a bad thing.

Conversely, picnicking and bushwalking are useful. They either bring people together in a relaxing atmosphere and encourage meaningful bonding and contact, or if they are done alone they create an ideal opportunity to think about one's life (and other things) peacefully, calmly and with perspective. So there.

The New South Wales Golf Club has been there since 1925 and leases this choice piece of land from us, via the state government. You'd think they'd be so grateful to have it that they'd welcome any of us legal owners on for a hit. Not so: 'As a private members only golf club we do not offer 7 day a week public access times. Subject to special events, we do, however, allow limited public access during weekdays only. No weekend times are available unless invited by a member.'

And if you do jump through those hoops and make it on to the course, you'd better make sure you behave: 'Golfers are expected to arrive at least 15 minutes before their allotted tee time and must report to the Professional Shop before tee off. Names must be entered in the visitor's book and identification passes will be issued for all players . . . No Metal Spikes. Strict Dress Code.'

Yes, sir! Golf's dress code is designed to make those playing it look as if they are not actually playing a sport at all but are instead accountants on their way to a barbecue. The dress code is proof that golf is not a real sport because real sports do not have dress codes. Weddings have dress codes, visiting the Governer-General has a dress code, but sports do not. One of the great things about sport is that it gives us all an opportunity to wear our daggy Adidas, Mitre 10 and Dire Straits Brothers in Arms Tour t-shirts that would never otherwise see the light of day. No one has ever been turned away for a game of squash, touch football or netball because their shorts didn't have a belt. It's stupid and pretentious.

So we didn't pop in for a game of golf.

Eventually, after what seemed to be at least 2 kilometres, we reached the top of the hill, only to find it was still 700 metres to

Henry's Head. We were only at about Henry's stomach. We walked along the ridge for a few minutes then stopped at a lookout. We could see for miles: Botany Bay, Cronulla and the ocean. Magnificent, head-clearing stuff. It seemed impossible Henry could provide a view that was any better so, after soaking up as much of it as we could, we turned around.

On the way back we passed a fiftyish couple.

'Lovely day,' I beamed.

'Would be it if it were downhill,' said the man in a thick English accent. I've said before that I hate stereotyping, I think it's wrong, but he was a whingeing Pom.

We returned to the beach and sat at the west end, nearest to, but invisible from, the road with our back to the rocks. A beach is a beautiful thing. One so close to home surrounded by bush rather than carparks and buildings is even better.

Bibi and I had a paddle and made friends with another dad and daughter. Both girls squealed in delight as they were swung about and dipped in the sea and both were so totally absorbed in the exhilaration of it that it made me wonder why we seem to get worse at enjoying the moment as we get older. People study yoga and meditation for years to learn how to be 'in the moment', to focus on the present rather than the past or the future, but all they are really trying to do is reclaim a lost skill, because at age one we were all expert at it.

I pulled Bibi up to eye level. 'What's your secret?'

She just giggled.

Next to us, three-quarters of a New Zealand family had stripped down to swimmers and run into the water while Mum checked the sleeves of her long-sleeved shirt were buttoned down and covered any exposed flesh with sunscreen. There was role reversal going on in the water. While the two kids, about ten and eight, lazed belly-down in the shallows, Dad ran madly about, throwing a frisbee into the sky then charging off through the waves to dive after it.

At one point he turned to the rest of the family and yelled fiercely, 'Come on! Make the most of it!' Even without the accent, it was obvious that this family was on a proper holiday, not just stealing a morning away from routine. While the rest of us were just grateful not to be working or doing chores at home, the Kiwi adults had the grim look of those under pressure to enjoy every single minute of their expensive holiday. They were going to have fun, dammit, whether they liked it or not.

Eventually, we picked ourselves up to move on. After an hour on the beach, standing was like weightlifting. On the way up to the road we passed a young guy carrying a boombox on his shoulder, blaring out the same radio station the builders listened to. He had the speakers facing away from his ear.

'Hey, did you ever think that maybe some people don't want your radio shoved down their ears? 'Cos if you haven't ever thought that, then maybe you should. Now.'

Luckily he didn't hear me because the radio was loud and I was speaking very softly (actually, you'd probably call it whispering) with my hand in front of my mouth as if I was coughing. Luckily for him, I mean.

Up the stairs from the beach and across the road (west) is a park overlooking Botany Bay. In the middle of it is what looks like the top 6 metres of a castle sticking through the grass. A perfect stone square with turrets on top. A bit of Medieval Europe in the south is how the real estate agents would describe it. From the top you would get a view of the whole entrance to Botany Bay. Presumably it was used to keep watch for intruders. But who? Russians, refugees, Kiwis, Japanese, sharks, communists, terrorists or one of the other groups we have been paranoid about in the past. In fact, it's a monument to the priest

Louis Receveur, a member of La Perouse's expedition, who died and was buried there.

Bare Island lies a hundred metres south into Botany Bay, connected to the mainland by a wooden bridge. People were fishing on the little island, and there was an old fortress cut into one side. Apparently it was built in 1885 to guard Australia from possible attacks by Russia, but strangely the fortress faces not out to sea but back to land, as if they were expecting the attack to come from Sydney. Perhaps even back then they thought there were Russian spies within.

On our way back to our car we passed a car parked across the road from the park. Next to it was our friend with the boombox and another man. They weren't talking and indeed there would have been no point, because next to the car, set down in the middle of the road, was the boombox, speakers facing away from the car and blaring even louder than before. Perhaps he was employed by the council to provide noise. Maybe he job-shares with someone with a leafblower.

eleven
sticking our necks out

'Lucy?'

'Mm?'

'You know how you said we could stay at your parents' house when they went away in October?'

'Mm.'

'Have you actually asked them yet?'

'Not yet. But it'll be fine.'

'Right.'

. . .

'But, Lucy, do you think you could ask them?'

'I'll ask them.'

''Cos then we'd know, and it'd be good just to know.'

'Okay.'

'Do you feel awkward about asking them?'

'No. I just haven't got round to it yet.'

'Because if you do I could ask them.'

'I don't feel awkward.'

'Why don't you give them a call and ask them now then,

just so we know, you know.'

'Because it's midnight.'

'Right.'

. . .

'Have you asked your parents about us staying at their place yet?'

'Yes.'

'You have? What did they say?'

'They said it should be fine.'

'Great. Oh, that's great. Thanks.'

. . .

'Lucy?'

'You know when you said you'd asked your parents about us staying when they're away?'

'Mmm.'

'And you said they said that "it should be fine"?'

'Mmm.'

'What did they mean? Like, what does it depend on?'

'Nothing. Mum said it should be fine.'

'Yeah, but "should be fine". That doesn't sound like defiritely fine. That sounds like probably but maybe not fine. Maybe we should just make sure?'

'Do you want me to ring her now?'

'Yeah, that'd be great.'

'I'm not going to.'

'Oh . . .'

'Um . . . why not?'

'Because it's half-past midnight.

'Right.'

. . .

'Lucy?'

'Yes.'

'Did you check about the house?'
'Yes, it's fine.'
'Definitely fine?'
'Yes.'
'Are you sure?'
'Yes.'
'No should bes? Definitely?'
'Yes! Definitely! Okay!'
'Okay. I was just asking.'
. . .
'Have you got a key for your parents' place?'
'Yes.'
'Good.'
'Um . . . where is it?'
'Somewhere around.'
'Right. Maybe we should check. Like, what if you can't find it?'
'I'll find it.'
'But can you check before they go because if you can't find it then . . .'
'All *right!*'
'Thanks.'
. . .
'Their place has got an alarm, hasn't it?'
'Hey?'
'Your parents. They've got an alarm?'
'Yeah.'
'Do you know how to turn it off and on?'
'There's a code.'
'Right.'
. . .
'You know the code for your parents' place? Do you know what it is?'

'They'll tell me before they go.'

'But maybe we should find out now, just in case . . . don't you think . . . we should get it before they go? . . . Lucy? . . . don't you think we should . . . Where are you going? Why are you running . . . I'm just trying to make sure . . . LUCY . . . DON'T PULL YOUR HAIR . . . COME BACK.'

. . .

'Lucy.'

'Mmm.'

'I think I'm coping with the builders a bit better now.'

'That's good.'

'Do you think that?'

'Yes. I'm coping better.'

'No, I meant do you think *I'm* coping better.'

'Oh.'

'Do you?'

'Not really, no.'

'But I'm less stressed about it. Apart from when they use that big drill at number eighteen, or they do something on the adjoining wall at number twenty-two. Which they do quite a bit, actually. That still makes me stressed. 'Cos it's loud. And getting woken up by them. That still makes me stressed. But apart from that I'm more relaxed, don't you think? Mainly anyway. Not all the time but often. More than I was anyway. A bit. Don't you think, Luce? Lucy? . . . Lucy? Bibi? Are you awake? How do you think I'm coping?'

While our efforts to see bits of Sydney had begun as a desperate ploy to escape the builders, we were gradually getting used to them. The building wasn't any quieter, drilling and crashing noises were still our constant companions, and in fact now there was a third site, directly across the road. This lot had obviously discovered that about every fourth day we got a moment or two of silence when both number eighteen and number twenty-two were between crashes, and had started up a second-storey balcony-addition thingy to fill the hole in the noise market. But we had reached an accommodation with number eighteen about their radio, whereby they kept it up the back of their site away from our bedroom and so only flooded our living area with that variety of noise. That wasn't as bad because we had a stereo there and could fight back. It made it a fairer contest.

One morning there was a knock on the door. I opened it to see the foreman, blond-haired with a matching goatee and, like most of number eighteen's builders, a Kiwi. I knew his name was Johno because when you have lots of builders over the fence shouting at each other all day you soon learn their names.

'Hi. Sorry to disturb you, but I just wanted to know if you'd mind if we swept up the mess on your deck. Sorry, some stuff came over your fence yesterday and I would have come over and cleaned it up then, but you weren't here and I didn't want to come onto your property without your permission. So if it's okay we can clean it up now, or if not just let us know when's a convenient time.'

Holy shit. Was he naturally this nice or did every foreman have to do a course in 'sucking up to the neighbours after you trash their property' before they got their certificate?

'Now's fine. Thanks,' was all I could get out.

'Okay. Sorry to disturb you.'

As I shut the door, I wondered if he would have been that polite if we hadn't lodged an objection with council to the positioning of their big airconditioner. With that outstanding, they had an interest in keeping us onside. Or was I getting paranoid? Maybe he was just nice.

But if he was, that wasn't all good. Sure, if he was nice it would be easier to ask him not to drill outside our bedroom window at seven in the morning but the downside was that it made it more difficult to view the builders as a pack of devils who'd come to ruin our lives, and I found viewing them that way sort of comforting. It allowed me to feel it was all unfair and I was a poor helpless victim and one day they'd all be sorry. It was hard to maintain that view when, just as I was getting a good head of isn't-it-all-unfair steam up over the concrete they had splattered on the side of our house, Johno would appear and courteously ask whether it was okay if he washed it off now, or if I'd prefer that he did it tomorrow.

At number twenty-two the builders didn't even have a radio! I looked them up in the *Guinness Book of World Records* and sure enough there they were: Only Builders in the World Not to Work With a Radio On.

As we came to the end of September, we looked forward to and savoured the quiet weekends, or more usually just the quiet Sundays as they often worked Saturdays, but after a few weeks we didn't feel we needed to escape the house every single morning. Sometimes we'd just sit tight, turn the stereo up and pretend they weren't there. As September drew to an end I wondered if we'd really get around to moving to the in-laws.

Then, at the start of October, we bought a house.

We knew we wanted to move someday. A three-level backyard with sixteen possible things to fall off was fine for a crawling baby but would be tempting fate with a walking toddler. When the building started it had motivated us to have a bit of a look around. We saw a house in the same street that was a bit bigger and had a horizontal backyard, talked to the bank and realised that we couldn't really afford it. Still, we may as well go to the auction as practice, for when we were serious.

It was at a posh hotel in the eastern suburbs, on the second floor in a plush conference room. All the people from the real estate agents were in black tie. Auctions, like golf, apparently have dress codes. They were trying to create a sense of occasion. We shuffled in and I thought I was being clever picking a seat up the back, so we'd get a view of everything and know exactly what was going on. But we had no idea what was going on. The people in black tie knew what was going on. The house we were interested in was second on a list of eighteen. It took a long time to get a first bid which, when it came from the other side of the room, was only about $30,000 under our limit. We thought we were gone, but Lucy found a voice and threw a bid in. Just for practice. The other side popped another $10,000 without hesitation. We were $10,000 away from our limit. Lucy looked at me. I shrugged. I didn't know what to do. She bid. We waited for the other side to respond. They didn't. For anyone to respond. No one did. I started to sweat. I sat there calmly, which wasn't what I wanted to do. What I wanted to do was to get up and run screaming out of the room, but I thought that might be interpreted as another bid. Auctioneers call bids on nasal hairs rustling in the wind. We waited. So did the auctioneer. He waited a very long time. Nothing. He passed the house in. It hadn't reached its reserve price. The agent approached and beckoned us outside.

He was a kind, gentle shark with a limp. In black tie. He told us that he liked us, that we seemed nice. He said he didn't want to sell it to the other people who had bid, because he didn't like them. They were playing silly buggers. He'd much prefer it if we got the house because we were nice.

He was warm. The fact that he liked us made me feel warm. We didn't know what was going on and here was this seasoned pro who said he liked us and wanted to help us. How lucky was that?

We had to help him to help us, though. Of course. That made sense. If we could stretch a bit more, make an offer a bit more than our final bid, it would just give him something to go back to the owner with and then everything would be all right and the house would be ours.

I told him we'd love to but we'd reached our limit.

'Limits,' he said, nodding his head. He understood. He knew about limits. When I bought my first house, he said, I had a limit and you know what? I went way over it. It was scary, he said, but it was the best move I ever made. Limits are things that hold scared people back from achieving their dreams, he said. If only we could stretch a bit, he said, just a bit, then the house would be ours. That. House. Would. Be. Ours. And we would live happily ever after. And the other couple wouldn't live happily ever after. We would win and they would lose. And he wanted us to win because he liked us. But we had to help him. If only we could just stretch a bit.

We stretched a bit.

'Just a bit more,' he said, 'and they'll grab it, I'm sure.'

I shook my head.

'Come on, James,' he said, 'what's wrong with you?' Was that a hint of contempt in his voice? He sounded like an exasperated abseiling instructor who couldn't quite persuade a student to go over the edge. He knew it was for the best, he knew things would turn out okay, but we were frustrating him with our lack of nerve. I could tell he was disappointed in me. I'd let him down. He liked us, he was trying to help us, and here we were throwing it all back in his face. Maybe soon he wouldn't like us any more and he'd offer the house to the other couple and they'd be the ones who got to live happily ever after.

What was I, a wimp? Wouldn't we regret letting this go for the rest of our lives? Were we the sort of timid, terrified

people who were too scared to ever do anything? No. God-
dammit we weren't.

We stretched a bit more.

Then he looked earnest, impressed. He knew it was a big
step. It had taken nerve but we hadn't failed him. We had
come through.

'I think we've got a shot at it,' he said, softly, intensely, like
you might, in war, say, 'I'll circle round the back and attack from
the rear.' He said 'we', not 'you' because he was on our side. He
turned, still looking earnest, but as he walked over to the owner
I bet he was smiling.

So we bought the house.

He returned with the owners and there were smiles and
handshakes all round. The owners were smiling hard to hide
their disappointment at not getting as much money as they
wanted, and we were smiling hard to hide our fear at suddenly
plunging deep into debt. Only the real estate agent's smile was
genuine—he was on commission.

The catch, and the only reason we had been able to afford the
house, was that there were tenants with a lease in place for
another year. So even buying a house didn't give us an escape
from the builders.

That night, 3 a.m.

'Lucy?'

'Yes.'

'You awake?'

'Yes.'

'Have you been awake all night thinking, "What have
we done"?'

'Yes.'

'What have we done?'

'I don't know.'

'Can we afford it?'
'I don't know.'
'Are you scared?'
'Yes. Are you scared?'
'No.'
. . .
'Lucy?'
'Yes?'
'I am scared, really.'
'I know.'
'Oh.'
. . .
'Lucy?'
'Mmmm?'
'I'm really scared.'
'Mmmm.'

I kept trying to tell myself how clever we'd been. In the middle of a property boom it was smart, wasn't it, to borrow a heap, buy a tenanted house and then in a year's time sell our original house because in the meantime our original house would have appreciated by so much that we'd end up owing not all that much.

Unfortunately, pretty much the day after we bought the house the property bubble burst and our strategy of buying before we sold started to look shithouse. My estimates of what we could sell our current house for went from looking conservative to frighteningly optimistic very quickly. I started to panic and found out that instead of using spare mental space to plan places to go and things to do, I spent the day doing maths—endless financial calculations involving interest rates, capital gains tax, agent's commission, land tax, rent, stamp duty, salary, income tax and lawyers' fees whirled around in my mind again and again.

I had visions of the property market turning sour, of our place depreciating 20 per cent and being left having bought a new place when everything was expensive and having to sell our old place when everything was cheap, resulting in a debt that was way too big. We would be the only couple in town to have lost money in the property boom. Those idiots who had bought at the top of bubble, and sold after it popped. Middle-class morons.

Or even worse, what if no one wanted to buy our house? No one at all. Ever. How could I ever have thought it was worth that much? It's got a vertical backyard. Our house could be on the market forever. It could be the one house in Sydney that will never ever sell. Never ever. It would be famous. 'Look,' the tourist guides would say as their bus drove past, 'that's the house that will never sell.'

For the first time ever I read the financial pages. Every day in every paper there was a different expert opinion about what would happen, just as at the casino at every table there is a different expert who can tell you which way the cards are running or the dice are rolling. And while just like at the casino all the experts confidently and adamantly disagreed, somehow it was reassuring to read a convincing and well-written analysis, because it suggested that there was some science to it all, that we weren't just playing a giant game of roulette.

I could feel that old, gnawing, anxious feeling beginning to eat into my days again.

We decided the only safe thing to do was to sell number twenty as soon as we could and rent somewhere until the tenants' lease was up. Out the window went our plans of staying at Lucy's parents' house while they were away and out went our morning adventures. Instead, the next month was spent scraping and spac-fillering and painting and fixing and polishing and weeding and sweeping and lugging dirt and chucking out crap and hiding the rest of the crap that we couldn't quite bring ourselves to chuck out in the roof, and trying to work out what optical tricks we could play to make our house look bigger, our garden flatter and the building sites next door less like building sites next door.

By the end of the month the house looked really nice. Funny how you only get it looking good when you're about to leave. You know how it is. You move in with big plans, you have an initial burst then one day you get sick of it and leave the rest until later. We had left plenty until later.

We talked to real estate agents. It's a waste of time asking a real estate agent advice about when's the best time to sell. Whatever the circumstances, their answer will be 'Now', because they want your money now. If you have ugly building sites either side of your house they will say 'Sell Now'. If a law was passed saying that in two months' time every house will treble in value and anyone who sells before then will be put to death they will still look you sincerely in the eye and tell you that it is in your best interests to 'Sell Now'. They want your money now.

So we spruced our place up, put it on the market and even had people through a couple of times. But then interest rates went up and no one seemed to want to buy anywhere anymore, much less a semi with a sloped backyard next to constant drilling. We pulled the pin and decided to wait.

It was only when we made this decision that I thought about how different my October had been to my September. In September we had gone exploring and discovering. In October we had been sensible, played it safe and learnt little. September had been about going out and looking. During October we stayed in and painted. September was about parks, streets and faces we had never seen before, and October was about interest rates, scrubbing walls and meeting real estate agents we never wanted to see again. September was about enjoying being somewhere unfamiliar, October was about trying to get secure at home. September was broadening, October was narrowing. September had been about the moment, about now, October was about the future. In the end, September was fun and October wasn't.

The difference in what we did in those two months had a big effect on me. September had been interesting, exciting and stimulating. Empowering too, in that we had worked out how not to let the builders make us miserable. But in October I became so preoccupied with doing the right thing financially and improving the value of our prime asset that the simple enjoyment I had derived from our expeditions ebbed away. I went back to plotting and planning.

I fell back into the bad habit of worrying; worrying about the money, worrying about getting the house fixed up in time, worrying about whether buying the other house had been a mistake. I worried about whether I'd have time to go and buy more paint and finish doing the bathroom door before I had to go to work, and about whether the paint tin would have one of those really difficult-to-open lids that took twenty minutes' levering with a screwdriver to open. I worried about whether I'd even be able to find the screwdriver to lever the tin open with, and about what, if I couldn't find the screwdriver, I'd be able to find to use instead. I worried about everything.

Once again, I worried to try to convince myself I had things under control. And the more I worried about one thing, the more I found others to worry about. So in September I didn't worry at all about my radio ratings going down and getting the sack, or about checking that my fly was done up five times before I got on the bus, or about whether any more Robbie Williams songs would be added to our play list, and if they were whether I would take a stand and refuse to play them. But in October, because I had all my worry synapses revved up and looking for action, I worried about all those things.

Toward the end of October I began to wonder why, having just in September discovered a great way to have fun, I had let it slip away. I realised how much time I'd spent thinking about things that gave me no pleasure—money, property and interest rates—and how far I'd drifted away from going out each morning and enjoying myself.

So in November we decided to get into it again. We weren't going to sell our house until next year, it had had its lick of paint, the building all around was still way too loud, so off we went.

And almost immediately all the money worries receded. They got back into their cages, into a controllable space where I could take them out, have a think about them, and put them away again. They weren't howling dogs running out of control through the house any more. They had their kennels, and I had the key.

twelve

storming the battlement

One of the differences that emerged in our choice of destinations was that Lucy preferred places with people and I preferred places with trees. Haberfield and Lakemba had been her choices, Manly and La Perouse mine. It's because she grew up in Sydney and I didn't.

Generally those who grew up in big cities have great difficulty believing that living, or even being, anywhere other than in a big city can be anything else but a monotonous hell. This attitude extends even to parts of the city they live in that don't look like a city, like the little bits of bush we found in Manly and La Perouse.

'But what do you do there?' they say.

'You just relax, look about.'

'But why?'

'Because it's nice.'

'Why?'

'It just is.'

'But is there a café? With *real* coffee?'

The only places that people who grew up in a big city want to move to are bigger cities. Sydneysiders want to move to London or New York, Melbournians want to move to Sydney and Adelaideans want to move to Sydney, Melbourne or Dubbo (Dubbo isn't actually bigger than Adelaide, it just has more of a buzz).

While an Adelaidean moving to Sydney is farewelled like a brave hero going off to war (mothers fear the worst and cry, friends envy their courage and hate themselves for staying home), a Sydneysider who moves to Adelaide will slink out of town as anonymously as possible. In the months leading up to their departure, friends will avoid the subject in the same embarrassed way that lawyers avoid mentioning property in front of their one colleague who is renting, and behind the departee's back will shake their heads sympathetically and share an understanding that this is a person who just couldn't quite cut it in the big smoke. Those who remain have, by implication, their belief that they can cut it reinforced. It makes them feel better.

This is the case even if the reason the person is moving from Sydney to Adelaide is because they got promoted from filing clerk to head of a multinational company whose head office is in Adelaide (as unlikely as that sounds). The reason for the move isn't important; it's the geographical fact of it that signifies social doom.

It's not a phenomenon peculiar to Australia. I know of a New Yorker who was walking along Bondi Beach (and Sydney is to New York what Adelaide is to Sydney) who said, 'So what is this lifestyle thing everyone keeps talking about?' His companion silently opened his arms out to the waves and the sand.

If you ask a big-city dweller if they would ever consider leaving the city they always bluff you with something like: 'But there's so much to do here . . . the restaurants and the theatres . . . And you can go to the beach whenever you like.'

Ask them when they last went to the beach or the theatre.

'Well, not for a while, but see, the point is that I know I could whenever I wanted.'

The truth is that they are city people, they have always been city people and for them living anywhere else would be weird and scary. They love feeling sophisticated and urbane in the same way that people who live up the coast love feeling relaxed and warm, and people who live in the country love feeling straightforward and knowledgeable about the weather. It's a good system. Everyone feels superior in some way. Except those who live in Adelaide.

I've lived in Sydney for eighteen years and have, therefore, been largely socialised into believing what the natives believe, that Sydney is superior. But there is still a small non-Sydney part of my mind fighting for survival, desperately trying to make me believe that one day I will move up the coast and live five minutes from work and two minutes from the beach and know everyone in town and that everyone in town will be interesting even though they don't live in the city.

I had realised that Lucy and I had different attitudes to the city three years earlier when she visited New York to see her sister. When she'd asked me if I wanted to go I'd said that the last place I wanted to go when I was on holiday was one of the biggest cities in the world.

When she returned I arranged a 'let's get to know each other again' walk from the Spit Bridge to Manly, a wonderful three- or four-hour walk around the harbour that keeps emerging from bush at spectacular lookouts. We were looking back over the sail-filled harbour toward the city, the Opera House and the bridge, at one of the most spectacular views, surely, in the world when Lucy said, 'You know, I really miss New York.'

Vive la différence. The only way, I think, that I'll ever be able to get her to want to live anywhere else in Australia but Sydney is to find a hypnotherapist who works.

So the Garigal National Park was obviously my choice. It's halfway up the North Shore and runs either side of Middle Harbour Creek, a body of water that eventually widens to become Middle Harbour and then, after it has run under the Spit Bridge, Sydney Harbour.

There were at least three reasons Lucy was in a bad mood when we got there. One was that she wasn't particularly excited about our destination. Another was that she hadn't been impressed in the car when I had pointed out, with not much tact at all, that I thought she was a shithouse navigator whose efforts were on a motivational par with mine when I gardened for Mrs Marshall. The third reason she was in a bad mood was that I had deprived her of coffee.

Lucy had wanted to stop for a coffee on the way, but (a) I was conscious that we only had five hours to get there, have a look and get me back to work; (b) I resented the fact that having an instant coffee at home before we left wasn't good enough for her (although, as an ex-addict, I knew full well how much better the real stuff was); and (c), most importantly, I resented the fact that I had gone through all the pain of giving up and she hadn't.

Rather than say any of this I used delaying tactics, trying not to drive past any coffee shops, and then if she did spot one playing dumb.

'There's one.'

'Where?'

'There.'

'There?'

'No. There!'

'Where? Oh, there . . . Is there somewhere to park?'

'Yes. On the right.'

'Where?'

'There.'

'Where?'

'There!'

'There? Oh *there*. Missed it. Sorry. Next one.'

This worked until we turned off Archbold Road (just before it lost its identity and became the romantic sounding Eastern Arterial Road) into East Lindfield and then it was too late. No more shops and no time to go back. As Lucy gradually became aware of this, she gradually got the shits. (Having just re-read this, I think I might be a selfish bastard. Imagine what I'd think if I read her version.)

Here, in fact, is Lucy's version: 'I thought it would be nice to have a walk in the bush, but even nicer to have a fortifying cup of coffee just to get a burst of energy beforehand. Bibi hadn't slept much the night before so I needed a bit of a boost. James was playing dumb whenever we passed a café because he didn't want to stop. On balance was he a selfish bastard? The answer is yes.'

So the motion is carried two votes to nil.

East Lindfield is a leafy, well kept North Shore suburb that looks as if no one between the ages of eighteen and 40 lives in it. There are trees in every backyard and most front ones, the houses are big and affluent, and the only noise comes from birds. It feels safe, but also 'quiet, too quiet'. The streets are empty during the day, and I doubt if it gets any busier at night. People rarely leave the house except by car. It's the downside of there being lots of space; everything is further away.

Several streets back onto the national park and our street directory suggested that off one, Ormonde Road (a tiny cul-de-sac, not really a road at all), a track led to the creek. When we arrived, however, there was a sign: 'Walking track is between 48 and 52 Carlyle Street'.

The track must have saved up and moved to a bigger block.

A bit more winding around and we arrived at a park the size of a vacant block between 48 and 52 Carlyle Street. A sign announced it as Seven Little Australians Park, which looked to be about the most it could have held.

We dismounted and loaded up or, as they say these days, got out of the car and got all our stuff. A track wide enough so I didn't have to worry about whipping branches out of my way and into Bibi's face led off from the back of the park. It turned right to run along the backs of houses while a dry, tree-filled gully fell away to our left.

We were walking downhill but I didn't notice. When you're walking downhill you don't. You just think you're walking. It's only later when you have to come back up that you realise how downhill it must have been on the way there.

It was boiling hot, well over 30 degrees, which gave us an excuse not to talk. Even without words Lucy radiated the shits. It wasn't just that she hadn't had her coffee, it was more that she realised that I had deprived her of it. She has the ability, without words or actions, to somehow project such an 'I've got the shits' aura that it prompts tip-toeing and whispers from anyone within a hundred metres. (Bibi excepted. She was outside both the intent and the effect of it.) Luckily she only unleashes the aura onto me when I deserve it. In fact I may well be the only person she ever unleashes it onto, because I think I'm the only person who ever gives her the shits. Whereas I'm far more balanced. Lots of people give me the shits.

The track wound down the hill and the bush got denser. After ten minutes we arrived at a thin little creek that didn't look like it could ever get big enough to become a river, let alone a harbour. Not that the water was going anywhere. I threw a little bark boat in to amuse Bibi and it hung around as if tied to a buoy. A wooden bridge led us over it, then we turned left and followed the creek in the direction we thought was probably downstream. The trees closed in, and the shade kept us not exactly cool, but slightly less boiling.

But just as the boy becomes a man, the foal becomes the horse and the demolished rubble next door will hopefully soon become a completed house, within five minutes that muddy little creek had joined and become a big bold river 50 metres wide. The track had headed inland so at first we only caught glimpses of it, but then it emerged 20 metres above the bank. We were high enough to see a mile or two upstream. It was another big beautiful view.

Across the other side was bush broken by a picnic ground, fishing spots, a roped-off swimming area and one of those pseudo river beaches. Tragically, no swimming spot on our side. In fact we couldn't even get down to the water, thick brush and swampy mud barring our way.

The track cut into the river's steep bank and swung right and south toward the harbour. I kept up as good a pace as I could to try and get out of the aura's range. Projecting it seemed to drain Lucy's energy and she fell back. After ten minutes of pure river and bush view we rounded a point. Ahead the river widened and stretched forward, on either side scrub rose steeply to surrounding hills and there, right in the middle of it all, was Warringah Road, whooshing cars over the river and up the other side. It looked incongruous in the same way one lone inner-city tree hanging onto life through cracked pavement and surrounded by concrete, metal spike fences and street signs does.

A bearded dragon sat up on the path and watched us approach. When Bibi and I were within a few steps it casually sauntered off the path into the scrub. No panic, it clearly knew that once off the path it was safe from us. A minute later we saw another, then another. Nine in a hundred metres, either scuttling across the track, or reluctantly moving from where they had been sunbaking as insurance in case we turned out to be out to get them.

Eventually the track came to, and went under the Roseville Bridge. The foundations, inevitably, were graffitied. 'Stop the War!' was scrawled in metre-high black letters. It was hardly going to make a big political impact tucked away like that. Still, the war did seem to have stopped so maybe it worked. Unless they were talking about a different war.

On the other side of the bridge was a park into which I collapsed and released Bibi. It was a lovely location and the walk had been just the right distance, but the tension between Lucy and me had taken the gloss off the morning, especially because a nagging guilt kept reminding me I had caused it. Half my brain was relaxed by the surroundings while the other half was going over what had happened and trying to work out if it all really was my fault. When Lucy arrived I set about building a bridge. I'll spare you the details except to say that even selfish bastards can sometimes admit they are selfish bastards.

Then I explored a bit further downriver. A path from the park led around a corner and opened onto a beach. Still a river beach, but a long one, stretching far down toward the harbour, and with people lying on it as they do on a proper beach.

I backtracked and convinced Lucy it was worth the effort and soon we were all paddling in the shallows. Then we lay and lounged until eventually I offered to go back and bring the car around to the road I suspected was just above us. It wasn't an entirely selfless gesture for, while the bridge had been built, it was still rickety.

I headed up some stone stairs and found that indeed there was a road above, then came back down to the river and headed back along the path, setting a cracking pace. The relaxed part of my brain took over completely. Walking was just enough of an activity for it not to feel any pressure to think about anything else. The idea of money or work or chores being at all worthy of thought seemed ridiculous. The fact that I was walking very fast on a very hot day was enough to create self-worth. Surely a man who could do that would find any other problem trifling by comparison. I spotted a distant fisherman over the river and, following the rule that the less densely people are crammed together the more friendly they are, shouted and waved. He didn't hear or see, or if he did, ignored me because he thought I was weird. I strode on, confident of my ability to stride on, past the river, into the trees and then over the stationary tributary, heart beating faster, sweat dripping but pace unslackened. I felt disconnected from my everyday life, away from all its little hassles. I knew they still existed, but they seemed far away, and I more able to deal with them because hell, I was a man who could walk fast on a very hot day.

Then I hit the hill. The one I didn't notice on the way down. The trees spread out, shade retreated and the sun beat down. It was steep, much steeper, surely, than before. Had there been a grader in, in the last hour? I heard a noise. A steam train? Around here? Surely not? No, it was my breathing. As my pace slowed, my breathing quickened. My striding became walking became trudging became shuffling. I felt weak. Spent. Hardly a man at all. I stopped. Shuffled on. Stopped. Staggered. Stopped. Eventually, painfully, I made it back to Seven Little Australians Park, collapsed into the car, started the engine and blasted the airconditioner. Nature: it's good for a visit but I wouldn't want to live there.

The street directory helped me work out where Lucy and Bibi were and I took off towards them. Five minutes later I was speeding over the bridge we had walked under, across to the other side of the river, thinking, *This is wrong*. Warringah Road is a fine multi-laned piece of road construction but unkind if you miss a turn-off. Ten minutes later I found a place to turn around and come back.

Eventually I got to the bottom of Babbage Road on the border of Roseville Chase (one of the few Sydney suburbs containing a verb) and Castle Cove and picked them up. We decided to follow Middle Harbour Creek on its journey toward Middle Harbour and so drove back up Babbage Road, turned left and wound our way along the point that is Castle Cove, the Australian suburb with the largest property price increase in 2003. The average median house price increased by 51 per cent in that year, from $950,000 to $1,439,000. Yikes.

It's a finger surrounded by water. Middle Harbour Creek opening into Middle Harbour lies to its north and east, Castle Cove (the water not the suburb) to its south. From the water, dense bushland rises up a few hundred metres to the central ridge along which streets run.

It's another church-quiet suburb full of big family houses with water views, or almost water views, and sloping back-yards. Most look nice and comfortable, but a million and a half each? You're not buying houses, you're buying status, specifically being on the North Shore with either a view of the water or more likely a view of houses which have a view of the water. Being near bush would up the value, too, but as with the water you're paying for view not use. It's dense scrub on a near-cliff.

Bamp Place, a little cul-de-sac on the north side of the suburb, offers a huge view looking back up the river to where we were. We could see the park, the beach and the second half of our walk. And the Warringah Road bridge.

The downside of Castle Cove is the vertical back and front yards—like ours in Bondi only here they are bigger, more expensively landscaped and better maintained. At the end of the cul-de-sac a suited man was backing his car carefully and terribly slowly up his steep driveway. It took him three minutes with directions from his wife, and he still scraped the bottom.

We drove over to the south side of the peninsula and looked south to the next point just a few hundred metres across the water; it was the other Castle, Castlecrag. Why not?

It was a lot further than a few hundred metres to drive there, though. We had to go all the way back along the Castle Cove point, then south along the main road and back east into Castlecrag. Which was good because if they had put in bridges connecting the tips of each point it would have looked terrible.

Both of the castle suburbs have pretty much one road in and one out, so in case of attack from the poor the residents need only block up the one spot to make themselves safe until their tinned oysters, well-stocked wine cellars and deluxe pet food run out.

It's easy to describe the North Shore as the North Shore and leave it at that, but the Castles and the other Middle Harbour suburbs, Middle Harbour and Northbridge, have their own distinct character. The North Shore that runs either side of the Pacific Highway from North Sydney to Hornsby is all about trees, big flat backyards, trees, tree-filled gullies, smart shops clustered around train stations, long driveways, trees, leaves, and big suburban house after big suburban house that look as though they've been transplanted direct from one of the American big-family, feel-good 1970s TV shows like *The Brady Bunch* or *Eight is Enough*.

In the Middle Harbour suburbs the houses run out along ridges to the ends of points. There are water views but very little waterfront (except in Northbridge) as the bottom third of each point is pure bush. No private beaches here. The architecture is more adventurous than on the rest of the North Shore, and it has to be because so many of the blocks slope steeply. You can climb up or down into the garden, but in many of them kids can't run wild without a helmet and abseiling equipment. Because everyone wants to be able to see the water, the houses stand up on huge stilts and peer over each other like a group of giant spiders looking down a hill.

Like Castle Cove, Castlecrag is shaped like a cigar and is surrounded on three sides by water. Edinburgh Road is the only way in and it runs from the main road all the way to the point. The shops are at the main road end, which is where we parked.

A sign on Edinburgh Road told us that if we turned right we would be walking towards The Rampart, The Parapet, The Battlement, The Bastion, The Bulwark, The Citadel and The Redoubt. I wondered if we should be carrying shields and crossbows. Had all these different parts of the castle been spread about Castlecrag like a giant jigsaw? No. We turned into a street and found that it didn't contain a bastion (a projecting part of a fortification), it *was* The Bastion. They were all, it seemed, just weirdly named streets.

A little way along The Bastion, a track turned off into the bush. We followed it and after a few minutes popped out into a clearing filled with tennis courts and racquet-wielding middle-aged women with sculptured hair, wearing all-white clothes and all-gold jewellery. Each wore a sun-visor. No hats, they'd play havoc with the perm.

The track continued back into the bush and the tennis courts vanished as abruptly as they'd appeared, as if they'd been a mirage, except that mirages are usually of things you want to see. It emerged at The Battlement, which is not a battlement (a notched parapet built on top of a wall) at all but another street, and we passed a classic example of real estatism on a sign advertising big spidery houses on a steep block: 'No Lawns to Mow, No Gardens to Tend'.

In real estate speak, every minus can be a plus. Not having a garden becomes a lifestyle feature. No doubt somewhere else in Sydney a cupboard was being advertised as, 'No Floorspace to Vacuum. No Bathroom to Clean. No Windows to Open'.

Running off The Battlement is The Citadel, supposedly 'a fortress in a commanding position in or near a city', but actually a short dead-end. It does, however, actually contain something castle-like, a house that looks like a small version of, or a part of, one. From the rough stone walls to the square shape and flat roof it looks like the real thing and if we were in Europe I'd think it was a genuine restored castle remnant. But we aren't so obviously it isn't. It must be one of the sixteen houses Walter Burley Griffin and his wife, the architects responsible for Canberra, designed in Castlecrag in the 1920s and 1930s. They designed the whole shape of the suburb, the idea being to incorporate as much of the native bush and landscape as possible, a novel concept at the time. It worked in that it's one of only a few Sydney suburbs in which, wherever you are, you see more trees and bush than houses and road.

The flipside is that, as with Canberra, what is sacrificed are places for people to bustle about and bump into each other in, and which provide a means to create a sense of community. In Castlecrag you'd have to make an effort.

Walt and Marion wanted to create a place where people could live in harmony with nature. Of course, if they had been really into this idea they would have designed tents and lean-tos rather than houses, and banned electricity and shops, but Castlecrag does feel a long way from the city. I certainly felt more in harmony with nature there than I did walking past a row of head-high front fences in Bondi.

But their ideas wouldn't catch on today, I'm afraid. They don't sit comfortably with the new 'build to the boundary' Sydney style of architecture. When you want five bedrooms and a void, it cuts down on the space available to integrate seamlessly with nature. How do you seamlessly integrate a double garage, giant airconditioning unit and home theatre?

Out of the front of the house Walt and Marion designed, at the roundabout at the end of The Citadel was a white-haired man cutting flowers (freesias, Lucy said) with a pair of scissors. I wondered if that was allowed if you're living in harmony with nature, or if you should wait until they die of natural causes before you take them away and put them in a vase.

'Having a look around are you?' he asked. His tone was suspicious, as if concerned we might be scoping the place for a raid. Unusual to do that carrying a baby, I would have thought.

He gradually thawed as it became obvious we weren't carrying crowbars or wearing gloves, and told us we must see Castlecrag's amphitheatre which he himself had helped restore. I was sceptical, given how un-battlement, bastion, and citadel-like The Battlement, The Bastion and The Citadel had been. What was the amphitheatre going to be, a sloping park with a bench?

He was adamant it was worth it, though, and directed us down a path back through the bush and behind houses. We emerged at The Bartizan (a small battlemented turret), turned right into The Bulwark (an embankment built around a space for defensive purposes), right again into The Scarp (a steep artificial slope in front of a fortification), then came to the corner of The Scarp and The Barricade (a war measure that isolates some area of importance to the enemy). They were all just streets. I wondered, though, if living among them would eventually have an effect, and you'd start watching out for gangs of Goths and setting passwords to gain entry to the kitchen.

At the corner of The Scarp and The Barricade was a lush gully falling down towards the water. On one side were rock seats cut into the bush slope above a levelled stage surrounded by trees providing acoustic support. It was a perfect amphitheatre. It left the one at Martin Place for dead.

It was built by Walt, Marion and the Castlecrag community in the late 1920s and early 1930s. Back then they held plays, study groups, gramophone evenings, seasonal festivals and lectures there. (Wouldn't you just love to go to a gramaphone evening?) There's your community space.

Now that it's been restored they once again hold poetry reading and lectures there. The temptation was too much for Lucy and she did a bit of *A Midsummer Night's Dream* as Bibi and I formed a supportive yet discerning audience. It was a powerful performance made even more moving by the lawnmower accompaniment in the second half.

We wound our way back up the point along more parts of castles—The Barbette (a mound of earth inside a fort from which a heavy gun can be fired over the parapet) and The Barbican (a portable toilet that can be taken to barbecues; no, not really, it's an outer fortification or defence to a city or castle) to The Rampart (an embankment built around a space for defensive purposes). There is only one street in this part of Castlecrag without an irrelevant castle name, Rockley Street. Rockleys don't have anything to do with castles. In fact Rockley isn't even a word. I thought the street may be a new addition but it was there on the original plans. Maybe the Burley Griffins ran out of castle bits.

The Rampart is like one of the steep, winding mountain roads you see in movies with someone in a red sports car driving too fast along it just before they lose control and crash. There were no cars driving too fast in Castlecrag, though. In fact we saw hardly any cars, and definitely no red sports cars, so the absence of footpaths wasn't a problem. The few cars we did see, in the middle of a cloudless day, all had their lights on for extra caution. It's that sort of place.

My time was running out and we weren't sure of the way back. If only there was someone to ask. But no. The streets were as empty as empty gets. Eventually we found a woman on the low side of the street in her front garden, gloves on and digging weeds with the radio on a sensible talk station for company. I asked how we could get back to the shops.

'What way did you come from?' she said.

I pointed.

'Well, you can just go back that way and you'll get there.'

'What about if we keep going this way?' I said, pointing the way we were going. 'We'd prefer to go back a different way.'

'Oh.' She looked at me as if she thought that was very odd. 'Well, you can get there that way too.'

You do get odd looks walking around Castlecrag. Not the sort of odd look we got (and gave) in Lakemba. Those were because we looked different. In Castlecrag we didn't look different. In fact we looked like a typical Castlecrag family except that I wasn't wearing boating shoes and my shorts didn't have a belt, and Lucy had no jewellery on and her Indian shirt wasn't quite leisurely aristocrat enough. And maybe we were a bit young—although I'm bald with glasses so that would have helped. (That may be terribly unfair. There may be street gangs, text-messaging, loud stereos in too-fast second-hand cars, lots of parties, messy ignored gardens and all the other clichés that arrive with a twenty to 30 population in Castlecrag. We were only there for a couple of hours. But we didn't see any of them.)

In Castlecrag we got the sort of look that suggests that whoever is doing the looking can in no way imagine why you would want to take a couple of hours to just walk around and explore Castlecrag, and that the idea of doing it for no better reason than to see what is there is entirely weird. It's not a place that seems to contain a wild spirit of adventure.

On the way back in The Postern (a small gate in the rear of a fort or castle) we saw another of those impressive castley houses, this one with parapets, and a Steiner school, which fitted neatly into the back to nature idea.

As we drove out along the one road in (which rather than Edinburgh Road should be called The Drawbridge) and waited at traffic lights to turn back onto the busy highway that would zoom us back to the city, it occurred to me that perhaps the castle theme in Castlecrag wasn't as incongruous as I'd first thought. Drive down The Drawbridge and you leave behind the rest of the world and replace its bustle and unpredictability with stillness and staidness and peace. You find nice, safe, normal people who you can be confident will never do anything weird. The odds of seeing an Arab or an African face or someone wearing a baseball cap backwards or a beggar or someone with holes in the jeans, either designer or otherwise, are about the same as they are of seeing a dolphin sitting in a kebab shop in Lakemba. Castlecrag is safe, secure and homogeneous. The old castles used walls to keep people out but today we have a different type of barrier, just as effective: money.

thirteen

the dealer's mum

Bibi and I sat up the back one morning and watched the tilers on the roof at number twenty-two. Both were dressed as 1970s tennis players, in t-shirts, really short shorts like they had back then, and Dunlop Volleys. Maybe it was fancy-dress day.

Roof tiling is the glamour job in the building world. Every job has a view and fresh air, you gain status from being higher up than anyone else and there is that alluring hint of danger provided by the fact that one slip means death or serious injury. And you're virtually boss free. No one down below can tell what you're doing, and even if the foreman did want to tell you off, it is virtually impossible to establish authority over anyone 6 metres higher than you. If you tilt your head back to see up onto the roof you can't shout properly.

Plumbing, conversely, is at the shit end of building jobs. They're often unrealistically happy, though, plumbers. When our drainage system was buggered up by an ambitious tree-root a couple of years before, the 62-year-old smiling Scotsman who rescued us advised us to stand back, then used a whizzing metal hose that he fed down the drain to unblock it. As he pulled it out, still whizzing, it flung shit (ours) all over him.

'Got the bastard,' he said with a huge smile. 'Ah ha, that was a tough one.' He wiped his sleeve across his face, smearing the shit over a wider area. 'Got to be careful in this game,' he continued cheerfully. 'Most of us get hepatitis in the end.'

The tilers worked at a leisurely pace, had English names like Pete and Dud and a conversational range as wide as sport.

'Davis Cup final's on soon,' said the one in the red shirt.

'Been on already, hasn't it?' said the one in the white t-shirt.

'No, no. Not yet. Not the Davis Cup final.'

'Yeah. The Davis Cup final. It's been on. We beat Spain.'

'No. That was last year.'

'No, I know it was on last year but I thought it had been on this year as well.'

'No, it hasn't been on. They had the semi-final.'

'Oh, I know that.'

'But they haven't had the final.'

'I know they had the semi-final.'

'But they haven't had the final.'

'I thought they had the final. After the semi-final.'

'No, that was the semi-final.'

'How could they have the semi-final after the semi-final.'

'No, I mean . . .'

'If you win the semi-final you go into the final. You don't go into another semi-final.'

'I know that but . . .'

'That'd be stupid.'

'I know that, but what you thought was the semi-final must have been the quarter-final.'

'Hey?'

'And after that, what you thought was the final was the semi-final.'

'What . . . you . . . thought . . . was . . . the . . .?'

''Cos they had the semi-final . . .'

'I know they had the semi-final.'

'But they haven't had the final.'

'I thought they had the final . . . After the semi-final.'

'No.'

'No?'

'Yeah. No.'

'Oh. I thought they had.'

'No.'

'No? Okay.'

Red shirt laid a tile. White rubbed his chin, then picked up another tile.

'The semi-final was the one that was just on,' said Red.

'Right. I've got it now. And we beat Argentina.'

'No. We didn't beat Argentina.'

'Yeah. Argentina. In the semi-final.'

'No. We beat Argentina in the quarter-final.'

'Did we?'

'We beat Portugal in the semi-final.'

'I thought we beat Portugal in the quarter-final.'

'No.'

'No?'

'No.'

'I thought it was the quarter-final.'

'No. We beat Argentina in the quarter-final and Portugal in the semi-final.'

'Oh. Okay.'

White handed the tile to Red. Red bent to place it.

'So who are we playing in the final then?'

Red stood up again, tile still in hand.

'Of the Davis Cup?'

'Yeah. 'Cos I thought it had been on already.'

'No. Not yet.'

'Who are we playing then?'

'In the final?'

'Yeah.'

'Fucked if I know.'

Red laid the tile. White pulled out a pack of cigarettes from his back pocket and offered one to Red. They both lit up and stood back looking at the seven tiles they had laid so far. Time for a break.

After a few minutes they continued laying with an accompanying conversation that began with trying to work out where exactly Portugal was ('I thought it was between Spain and France.' 'No, that's Andorra.' 'Where?') but soon found its way onto the merits of watching golf on TV. They only had the back section of roof to do, so even at their pace it didn't take long to lay the rows out. The tricky bit was the edge where each tile had to have a corner sliced off to fit exactly the space at the end of the row. Red brought up the tile shears, like a paper-cutting guillotine but for tiles, and without anything more than a quick glance at each space, cut each tile to a perfect fit. No talking in this bit, concentration was required.

Another smoko and then a bucket appeared up the ladder. It was on the shoulder of a third tennis player who did the dud job, mixing cement at ground level. He was the one the foreman could shout at.

Two parallel plastic lines 3 metres long, connected by four rungs so it looked like a ladder for little people, was laid down on the edge of the roof where the new and old tiles met. It formed a guide along which the cement was laid and then on top of it other bigger tiles that locked all the others into place.

All three were involved in this job and the conversation left tennis and moved to English soccer, specifically on what new players Arsenal had and who they had lost. Again, the emphasis was on getting the facts straight ('Hobbs has retired.' 'Retired? I thought they sacked Hobbs.' 'No they didn't sack him. He retired.' 'Did he? I thought they sacked him.' 'No.' 'No? Okay.') rather than on any sort of analysis or opinion. Still, maybe, when one slip can mean death, it's safer that way.

Two days later number eighteen's roof tilers arrived. Theirs was a far bigger job, a full mansion's worth of tiling, and they looked like they meant business. They were younger, in their twenties, and wore boardshorts, workboots and bare chests. They were fit and in a hurry, they didn't have time for small talk or smokos. And yet they didn't get things done any quicker, mainly because where old Red at number twenty-two had been able to cut a tile exactly to fit by sight and experience, the young-sters had to first slot each into place, then scratch a line across it at the right place, then take it out, cut tentatively along the line, slot it back in and finally bash it with a hammer because it still didn't quite fit. More haste, less speed.

Eighteen's tiles were black. What's going on with that? Ivan's plans showed a big airconditioning unit he wanted to put on his back balcony. Maybe if he got tiles a colour that didn't conduct heat (i.e. any colour other than black) he wouldn't need it.

If you say the word 'Cabramatta' to most Sydneysiders it brings to mind two things. One is its cultural identity, predominantly Vietnamese. The other is its curse, heroin.

Cabramatta is in the south-west of Sydney, just north of Liverpool, and is officially Australia's most multicultural suburb. About three-quarters of those living there were born overseas and four out of five people speak more than one language. I don't know what percentage use or sell heroin, but it's a lot less than that.

It's near Sydney's edge, at least at the moment, but there's nothing spacious or rural about it. To get there you used to have to battle along the Hume Highway through Ashfield, Yagoona and Villawood, but now coming from Bondi it's left into South Dowling Street at Moore Park and then you're whooshed traffic-light free south past the airport, then west out to Liverpool. You don't see anything except other cars, a toll booth and noise barriers that have various things painted on them that attempt, unsuccessfully, to disguise the fact that they are noise barriers. But it's fast.

At Liverpool we turned right and then a kilometre later right again into Cabramatta. The suburb carries such baggage that I half expected the light to immediately dim and to see shadowy figures lurking around lampposts and disappearing into alleys. But the geography and architecture of Cabramatta is inspired by neither its heroin culture nor its Asian influence. If all the people and some of the shop signs vanished there would be very little evidence to suggest that Cabramatta was anything other than an Anglo Aussie suburb or that its drugs of choice were anything other than the normal Anglo Aussie selections of booze and smokes. The Vietnamese influence didn't grow with and influence the architecture of the suburb, it arrived afterwards.

We parked a block from the shops and train station in a street full of shabby grey blocks of flats. No apartments here, or if there are they've been carefully disguised to look like flats to keep their value down. There was the odd house too, on blocks twice as big, but worth half as much, as those in the east. Most had bits of car somewhere in the yard. A front half, a stack of tyres, a back half, a whole one with no tyres. If only they combined resources they could make full ones that worked. Right in the middle of all the residentialness, for no apparent reason and blending in like an elephant on a train station, was a huge white-walled Russian Orthodox church emitting a strong smell of incense. It wasn't quite what I expected as a first impression of the centre of Australia's Vietnamese community. Maybe the connection was that citizens of both countries had fled the commies.

The centre of Cabramatta doesn't look like a bit of Asia in Australia, it looks like a lot of Asians in Australia, grafted onto what was already here. The shops, the streets, the layout, the mall, the carparks are all typical Anglo Australian suburbia. It's what's inside them that's different.

About 80 per cent of the faces in the streets were South-East Asian, mainly Vietnamese, but I didn't feel an outsider. It seemed a busier, more welcoming place than Lakemba but maybe it was our attitude again. Over the years we had been more exposed to, and had become much more used to, seeing Asians than Arabs and therefore felt less threatened by them. And we were bigger than most of them.

The shops don't look Asian from a distance but they do up close. There are restaurants and toy shops and newsagents and fabric shops and $2 shops and travel agents and all the other shops you find at every other shopping centre, but they all have an Asian feel. Which means what, exactly? Well, it's obvious in the restaurants with whole pigs being carried in and then hung dangling from the roof, and ducks and greens being chopped up by white-aproned men wielding machetes, but everywhere is a bustle and a busyness. In every shop the shelves are tightly packed, and close enough together that you have to squeeze your way down the aisles. There are as many goods in every place as can fit, not elaborately arranged to make the shop look and feel comfortable and elegant, but crammed together any old how. There are plain functional signs rather than elaborate neon banners. It's function, not fashion. No space or expense is wasted on making things look good, on marketing.

The effect is to create a sense of discovery. You can't just follow the signs to the item you want to find because it could be anywhere, and so shoppers graze from shelf to shelf, and on the way perhaps find something unexpected. The seemingly random disorganisation could, in fact, be a clever ploy to ensure that in looking for what you want you inevitably come across all sorts of other things you might decide to buy as well.

The fact that it is so obvious that money isn't being wasted on décor or banners or space suggests there are bargains to be had, too. A beautifully interior-decorated shop may be a great place to look around in but I wouldn't want to buy there. These are their antidote. It's like law firms: a foyer full of paintings and coffee tables may make you feel relaxed and comfortable, but when you get the bill you'll know how they were able to afford them.

The attempt to use every inch of space even extends to mannequins. One in a chemist shop was covered in every type of bandage there is—elbow, biceps, knee, thigh, head and about fifteen others—so that it looked like the world's most accident-prone statue. The only exposed bits were the toenails, painted red to show attention to detail.

There is specialisation in Cabramatta you don't see elsewhere. In the mall is a shop that sells only mangos, and near it a butcher that only does chicken. Maybe you have to get each magazine from a different newsagent and there's a separate pub if you want mixed drinks.

In a toy and electrical shop we came across a plastic truck, just big enough to sit in if you were a one-year old, for $35, jammed into a space between heaters and stereos, and thought about buying it for Bibi.

Okay, I thought, *this is Asia*. I'd been to Asia. I knew how things worked. The price tag was merely an invitation to negotiate. The art of the deal is an Asian delicacy. If you don't haggle they don't respect you. It's how they do things. As I suspected, it wasn't long before the Vietnamese owner approached.

'You want truck?' he said.

I knew my opening words would be vital. Too keen and he would know he had me. I affected disinterest.

'Maybe,' I said.

'Okay,' he said and turned and walked away.

'Err . . . yes we might want it.'

'Okay,' he said over his shoulder and kept going.

Perhaps he'd been in Australia a while.

As we moved out of the shop I tried again.

'We might get it on the way back.'

'Okay,' he smiled.

Outside the shop the fact that Cabramatta was truly multicultural and not just Vietnamese was underlined by the presence of a Pommie street vendor selling $2 t-shirts.

Our progress was slow. Bibi had decided she'd had enough of being carried. She wanted to walk. She wasn't good at it yet but she was keen. She would fight her way out of our arms as if from the clutches of an arch villain and stagger off determinedly in whatever direction we weren't going, forcing all the busy bustlers to dodge her.

I don't know why there's an extra bustle that seems particularly Asian. Chinatown has it too, a sense that life is loud and busy and crowded. People don't stroll, they rush, and every conversation seems to involve talkers who are extremely adamant about whatever is it they are talking about. Two people meet and immediately gesture and speak as if they are arguing. They are probably just saying, 'Hi. How's the family?'

There are reminders of Cabramatta's other side, too. A sign reads 'Townsafe: this area is under constant surveillance'. I wondered if it was from cameras or people but when I looked around couldn't detect scrutiny from either. Across the road we spotted a drug dealer, surely he had to be, a twentyish Asian man lurking suspiciously outside a video game parlour. Why suspiciously? Well, he was wearing a beanie for one. On a bright spring day. Very sus. He probably had fifteen balloons of heroin tucked up under his hat. And he was chewing gum. A clear sign of nerves. Plus he kept glancing up and down the road.

We kept going, and ten minutes later he walked past us, smiling and holding the hand of an older woman who looked suspiciously like she might be his mother. I'd either got it wrong or he'd reformed pretty quickly. He'd even got rid of the gum.

In fact, apart from jumping to the wrong conclusion about him we saw no evidence at all of Cabramatta being the heroin capital of Sydney. No junkies, no needles, no dirty alleys, no young men wandering in the direction of pawn shops carrying stolen video recorders under their arms and no outraged television crews from *A Current Affair*. Actually, not even any pawn shops. Or porn shops. We didn't even see any cops. Maybe we were in the wrong place.

In fact we were. The police blitz on Cabramatta hasn't ended the dealing but it has forced most of it off the streets into houses, out of sight. If nothing else the place looks a lot better, and the sense of decay and grot that is present in other heroin hotspots like Kings Cross is utterly absent.

We looked for somewhere to have lunch. There was no shortage of choice. There are dozens of Vietnamese restaurants from '$3 lunch 5 great choices' up. Like the shops, none are too elaborate or expensive. The places are plain and functional. No one gives a stuff about the marketing or the look. As it should be, in my opinion. We chose a place that looked pretty much like all the others, a glass-fronted square with plain, tightly packed plastic tables. We were seated by the wall and a baby seat appeared without us having to request it. The fact that they'd gone to the trouble to provide it didn't mean Bibi would sit in it, of course. She was full of wriggles.

Even though the place was full, menus appeared and orders were taken in a third of normal restaurant time. I love that. I hate the waiting bit in restaurants. Waiting to get the menu, then waiting to order. You're all ready and then one person says 'Just another minute', and it's another quarter of an hour. If you get impatient in restaurants, eat Asian.

We tried to order by pronouncing the Vietnamese and I imagined the waitress rolling her eyes on her way back to the kitchen after trying to unmangle our words, thinking, 'The numbers are right there next to the dish. Why can't they just say the bloody numbers?'

In a parallel universe I am a waiter in an Aussie restaurant in Saigon, gritting my teeth as Vietnamese customers try and pronounce 'Grilled chops with peas and spuds'. 'For chrissakes, just say number 26.'

The food appeared in moments. It fits, the fast service, into the busyness and functionality of Cabramatta. The restaurant was all about the food, getting it and eating it, a refreshing change from trendy eastern suburbs places that look more like fashion and furniture boutiques than places to eat, and where more care is taken draping the asparagus over the veal at exactly the right angle than cooking it.

Our food was fantastic. Chicken noodle soup sounds like a pretty functional dish. You can get it out of a packet and the ingredients are pretty standard. Chicken, noodles and soup, plus a few greens tossed in. Yet this was as tasty and satisfying as any posh restaurant snazzy dish described as braised, poached, sautéed or any of those other words restaurateurs use to attach snobbiness to what is essentially fuel. Those places make food that looks like a work of art and tastes okay. Here was food that looked okay and tasted like a work of art.

Each mouthful was a joy. It was more chickeny and more brothy than any other chicken brothy thing ever. It had enough comforting warmth to be nurturing, yet enough spice to keep things interesting and there was exactly enough of it. The end of the bowl was just far enough away to make reaching it neither a disappointment nor a relief. I wouldn't be walking away hungry nor would I be staggering out painfully carrying a bloated gut.

The freshly squeezed lemon juice set if off beautifully and together they were exactly $10. By the time we left, 40 minutes after we'd arrived, we were officially content.

Cabramatta itself was as disarming as that restaurant. We walked in uncertain, we immediately felt comfy and interested and we left satisfied. It seemed a confident place, busy but not tense, and I wondered if that was at least partially because, while it had only recently become a Vietnamese suburb, it had always been a multicultural one. German, Italian and Yugoslav migrants established it, then in 1975 the first Indo-Chinese refugees arrived.

They had fled war and hunger and most had had to cope with a lot, and a raft of welfare and assistance services sprang up around them to help, some government-run, some not. Seeing what a vibrant community has grown up from those who arrived carrying fear and uncertainty and not much else seemed to underline how much has changed in the way we treat those who come here today fleeing the same things.

If the Vietnamese asylum seekers had spent their first one or two years here locked up, how much more difficult would it have been for them to adjust and prosper? And if, when released, they had only been given the uncertainty of a temporary protection visa (as refugees are now)—which lasts three years and then has to be re-assessed to see if the holder deserves further protection—how much more difficult would it have been for them to commit to their new home, to put down the roots that so obviously exist in Cabramatta?

The children who arrived here in and after 1975 would now be adults in the prime of life. What long-term effects would the detention system that exists today have had on them? We don't know, of course, but we might in twenty years.

With these thoughts in mind we decided to take a trip down memory lane on the way home to a place that a decade ago I had visited almost every week for two years: the Villawood Detention Centre.

When I had finally realised that corporate law was not for me I sent round after round of increasingly desperate letters to criminal law firms begging for a job. Eventually I got an interview with one and as soon as I walked into the interview I knew I was in the right place. The boss had jeans on, his legs crossed and his shoes up on the table. A superficial impression, sure, but after coming from the tight-arsed formality of the big end of town it felt right.

I got the job, in part because of my desperation. The boss said they couldn't pay me anywhere near the money a corporate firm could and I hit back with, 'Well, there's no way I'm going to turn this job down over money.'

The boss smiled and offered me the job on the condition I accepted possibly the lowest salary ever paid to a lawyer, about $10,000 a year less than I was on.

'Great. Great. Fantastic. That's great. Oh great,' I said.

His brow furrowed. I think he was wondering, given how hard I negotiated on my own behalf, what sort of a job I was going to do cutting deals for clients.

Half of the job was doing criminal law and the rest was doing immigration matters, mainly acting for asylum seekers. Each week I'd go out to Villawood and have conferences, usually via interpreters, with clients from Ghana and Sri Lanka and Iraq and Iran and Somalia and lots of other places. Detention wasn't a political issue then in the way it has become recently, and yet I wondered what the occupants did all day for months on end while they waited, waited and waited. I guess they just waited, waited and waited.

Even back then, there seemed to be a cynical attitude toward asylum seekers, as if people thought they had run away from their home, their family, their everything and risked their lives to get somewhere where they didn't know anyone—where they couldn't even speak the language—just for the pleasure of hood-winking us by pretending to be refugees. Economic migrants posing as refugees are incredibly rare. Here's why. To get here without a visa by boat or plane you have to have a fair bit of money to pay a smuggler and/or buy a ticket. If you have that sort of money, you don't need to flee for economic reasons. The people who would like to escape their country for purely economic reasons don't have the money to do so, and certainly don't have the money to get here. If they did, they wouldn't need to leave for purely economic reasons, because they'd have money.

The only remaining reason that I can think of to leave for somewhere where you don't know anyone, is fear.

It was Lucy's idea to have a look. It was pretty much on the way back from Cabramatta and she was shortly to be in a play set partially at Villawood. The detention centre is right in the heart of suburbia, separated from houses only by a fence, some parkland and a street. The old entrance I used to drive in was blocked up and we had to go round to the other side. As we circumnavigated we got a clear view of the detention centre from the back. The accommodation blocks were still there, seemingly unchanged, and the layout was as I remembered from ten years earlier. We passed the shops where I used to buy the paper before I went in, in case I had to wait (I didn't once think about bringing detainees in some foody treat to break their culinary monotony; at the time it seemed so important, for some reason, to maintain professional distance). We turned into a driveway and a hundred metres along pulled off into a dusty space full of parked cars. Behind us a red sports car pulled in containing a middle-aged Eastern Suburbs Mrs and a younger African man. They got out, each carrying big plastic bags of food.

'Shall we?' said Lucy.

'You go. I'll mind Beeb.' I gestured behind. She was asleep. Lucy got out and through the rear-view mirror I watched her follow other visitors toward a turbaned Indian guard.

I didn't want to go in. I didn't want to gawk and perve and stare. At first I tried to tell myself it was because it would be treating the detainees like zoo animals. But it wasn't that. Then I tried to tell myself the reason I didn't want to go in was that I'd done all my head-shaking ten years earlier and that having another look wouldn't achieve anything.

But that wasn't it either. The real reason I didn't want to go in was that going and looking again would remind me that, despite all my head-shaking, I hadn't done anything.

When those in detention were clients I had the satisfaction of someone who knows that while what they are doing might not be changing an entire system, they are at least doing what they can. It was frustrating work because the lawyer's role in a refugee application is limited and largely passive. I could sit in on interviews, make submissions and lodge appeals, but at the end of the day it all depended on whether the Immigration Department officer assessing the application believed the client, and whether what the client said was consistent with the information the department had from our Department of Foreign Affairs and Trade about their country.

I wasn't an advocate in the same way a lawyer running a criminal case was, I was an advisor and hand-holder. I rarely, if ever, felt I had influenced the outcome of a case. After two years I wanted to do more combative court work. I applied and got a job with legal aid based at a local court in Blacktown, where every day I was in court, on my feet, representing people charged with anything from shoplifting to murder to drug supply.

That was what I wanted to do. It was adrenalin rush from go to whoa and I quickly forgot about the detainees. Almost. As the years went by it remained an issue I cared about. But I never really did anything big. I never committed. There was no hiding from the fact that I had put my own self-interest ahead of fighting for a cause. I had ducked it and settled for comfort. Was that so bad? Sitting in the car watching Lucy walk toward the gate, I wondered what I should have done.

Then, when a little while later she came back, we drove away and I guess I must have started to think about something else.

fourteen
trimmed sideburns

The next day the renderers arrived at number eighteen. The house had been tied up with scaffolding, which made it look even bigger than it was, which was no mean feat. The renderers were crazy men who shouted all day. I say crazy, but they may have just been incredibly witty. All I know was that they shouted at each other in a language I didn't understand as if they were fighting, and just at the moment they seemed to have worked themselves up to such a pitch that I thought it was about to come to blows and knife fights, they would all burst out laughing hysterically. This happened in five-minute cycles all day. Loud, louder, louder, LOUDER, LOUDEST, laughing hysterically.

When they talked it was as loud as shouting. When they shouted it was so loud it peeled their rendering off the walls and they had to start again.

Rendering a house consists of madly flinging a concretey render mix vaguely in the house's direction until everything in the vicinity is covered in it, then smoothing down the render that has actually hit its target and trying to clean up all the rest that hasn't. Somehow, the render that misses manages to get not just on the ground directly under the wall being rendered, but also on the roof above it, the house next to it, the fence in between the two and pretty much everywhere else within shouting distance except—miraculously—the renderers. One thing they do learn at rendering school is to keep themselves clean.

Rendering is like painting: no matter how meticulously you try to cover up to ensure no paint can possibly get on the floor, table or grandparent you're trying to protect, once you remove all the layers of old sheets, newspapers, blankets, magazines, doonas, books and pillows you've been using as protection you will inevitably find that which you've been trying to protect has been spattered with paint. Even though it's impossible.

The renderers wrapped up Ivan's house in a giant tennis net so thoroughly that Christo would have been proud. It appeared impossible for any render to escape the netting. Their messy product was in a controlled environment and the only way any could have got over our side of the fence was if we'd snuck over and surreptitiously grabbed a handful while they were having a smoko. And yet for weeks after they had finished we kept finding little puddles of the stuff on the side of our house, on the ground, on our windows, even once in a coffee cup at the back of the cupboard.

'Did you sneak over and surreptitiously grab a handful while they were having a smoko?' I asked Lucy.

'No,' she said, and I believed her. It wasn't her. And it wasn't the builders' fault. Render, like paint, is just sneaky.

I went alone to Kings Cross, mainly because I wasn't sure that it would be a great place to bring a one-year-old. It was 1 p.m.

when I got off the train. I rose up the escalators and, via a long arcade, emerged into Darlinghurst Road about midday.

Kings Cross in daylight is like a drag queen without makeup. All the flaws the night hides are exposed. It's dirty and scummy. The footpaths have been nicely paved but there are cigarette butts all over them, and a smell of hungover morning-after garbage, as if last night there was a huge party. And last night was a Monday, the quietest night of the week. On Darlinghurst Road are bars, strip clubs, 24-hour convenience stores and fast-food joints with the odd chemist and newsagent thrown in to try to give the impression that it's a nice normal street, really. Although there is a library, bravely and uncomfortably nestled in between Porky's Nite Spot and the Risqué Adult Shop. Then McDonald's, of course, is full of people you suspect don't have their own kitchens, and who would never even give a moment's thought to trying one of the McSalads.

'Hey matey, can you lend me 40 cents?' A scrappily dressed fortyish man with a beard croaked at me.

'No, sorry,' I said hurrying past.

I objected to the word 'lend'. What repayment scheme was he proposing? Eight monthly repayments of five cents plus interest calculated by reference to commercial lending rates? I don't think so. I wondered how many times that day he would ask the question, and with what success rate.

On the streets were nervous-looking tourists searching for the quickest way out and probably wishing they had opted to stay in Homebush after all, backpackers wondering whether being 'right in the centre of the action' was really all it was cracked up to be and tossing up whether to leg it for that other hostel at Bondi, sailors whose gleaming white uniforms stood out as pretty much the only things that were bright and clean in the Cross, and, in the majority, the shabby. The shabby walked as if they were at sea, or on a trampoline—unsteadily—dressed in whatever they had and with a look on their faces that indicated that everything was pretty much fucked. As I wandered about Kings Cross I saw the same faces again and again. They all seemed to be walking in circles.

They were adamant, too, about everything. Across the road two men and a woman argued. They talked too loudly and gestured wildly. One of them flung his arm back behind him to point somewhere and nearly knocked himself off his feet. He threw out a leg to recover, staggered back a step, then shambled forward again, still just as adamant about whatever it was.

The fountain at Kings Cross is quite beautiful. The water billows out in all directions to form a sphere, but a fountain can't save Kings Cross; rather, you feel sorry for it, trapped in the grot. Down an alley from the fountain is a bookshop, but Kings Cross has had an influence: the front window is filled with porn magazines. Inside, *War and Peace* glances uneasily at the stack of *Penthouse* magazines next to him and hopes against hope that one day soon someone will buy him to get him the hell out of there. He still feels bitter about the man who picked him up and thumbed through his pages a few days before, then just as hope was brimming put him back down and grabbed a stack of pornos.

Outside a man on a streetsweeper vehicle drove past. Good luck, but just like cleaning up leaves in autumn, no matter how much you pick up there'll be just as much mess tomorrow.

Past the fountain and down the hill there are less shops and more apartments as Darlinghurst Road gets to the point where it turns into Macleay Street and Kings Cross becomes Potts Point. The personnel changes in this area, and a succession of fit-looking young men with arty bits of facial hair and wearing tucked-in tank tops, trendy pants and sandals passed me carrying their shopping or washing. There are hotels full of Japanese tourists, money changers, gourmet delis and posh restaurants, but the streets are still grey and drab.

I turned and headed back to the Cross, past the Wayside Chapel. The guy who'd asked me for 40 cents walked past again.

'Hey matey, can you lend me 40 cents?' If he recognised me from fifteen minutes before he showed no sign of it.

'No, sorry.'

He staggered off down the road.

An alley leads from the Wayside Chapel back to Darlinghurst Road. There are lots of alleys in the Cross, and I felt nervous walking down them even in broad daylight. I saw an autobank which reminded me of something stupid I did a few years ago, withdrawing $200 from an autobank in the Cross at two in the morning. Still, most people who are at the Cross at two in the morning do something stupid.

The alley had a computer and electrical shop that must have had very secure locks or else it would have been empty, and next to it a tattoo and engraving parlour. I hoped they never got their two functions mixed up.

Back up Darlinghurst Road, the way I had come, was a woman not really getting into the spirit of fast food as she sat in Hungry Jack's slowly sipping a drink and writing a letter.

A fake London double-decker bus drove by, with the bottom floor empty and the three people up top looking indifferent. It seemed to fit.

Another tattoo shop was right next to a glossy souvenir joint with its front window full of shiny didgeridoos. No one seemed to be inside either one. Across the road a woman was sprawled across the wide steps of an adult shop, frantically going through her handbag. At least I assumed it was hers. I walked past a strip club and a 20-year-old girl smothered in make-up whistled twice at me as the black-panted and t-shirted 30-year-old man beside her put his hand out in front of me and said 'Come on, someone, come on'. Gee it was tempting. The way he put his hand out, almost grabbing my arm, seemed particularly desperate and depressing. And pointless. Did he really think that that was going to change my mind? 'No, I won't go into the strip club. Hang on, he's got his arm out blocking my path. That must mean it's really good in there. Okay. I'm sold.'

Ten metres later I was propositioned again, this time by a smiley backpacker offering me a leaflet. To be consistent I declined again. Porky's Nite Spot was next. It was closed but loud music blared out of it and on the steps a middle-aged woman swayed from side to side, dancing. I didn't even get an invitation from her.

I saw snippets of lots of little dramas in the Cross that made me want to stop and watch what would happen next but I felt too conspicuous to do so. I got the feeling that if I looked too nosy someone might get a bit annoyed with me. Halfway back up Darlinghurst Road I did stop and leant against a tree to jot a few notes down in my notebook.

'Excuse me,' said a male voice. I looked up. Asian. Male. Thirty-something, clearly a drug lord. The triads were here. I was in trouble. Behind him another one, his number two. He'd be the one that did the dirty work and dumped my body in the harbour.

'Um, yes,' I said. Tried a smile.

'Are you wri-ing me a parking tick-e?' Behind him were two parked taxis. 'It is not a taxi stan, but me and ma frien were just havin a quick dri.'

'Oh. No. Sorry. No.'

'Okay.'

I hurried on, relieved to be alive, but perturbed that I looked enough like a parking inspector to be mistaken for one.

I turned left up Bayswater Road, and outside a pub saw two young men, both with shaved heads, t-shirts, backwards baseball caps and trackie-pants.

'I wanted to fuck him up, man. Fuck him up. He wouldn't fuckin' stand up to me. The fuckin' gutless prick. Fuckin' gutless, man.'

'Fuckin'.'

'Gutless fuckin' prick man. I woulda fucked him up.'

'Fuckin'.'

All very adamant. Who knows what it meant. I certainly didn't feel that either asking them to expand or staying to listen would have been a good move, but it was a fascinating tip of some iceberg.

I wound around to Kellett Street, which is the only part of the Cross that looks good in daytime. Cafés run down the street and trees on each side lean over and embrace above the middle. It should really be called an avenue.

Another flotsam-looking man walked past having an adamant conversation on his mobile phone. Except he didn't have a mobile phone. I snaked through more alleys back to Darlinghurst Road and while it was broad daylight and I was probably perfectly safe I didn't feel perfectly safe.

I was glad I hadn't brought Bibi. In fact I hadn't seen any kids at all in the Cross.

As I headed out of the Cross, south along Darlinghurst Road, a man staggered past me, heading without joy into the Cross. He stopped, fumbled in his pocket and dropped his wallet on the ground. He reached over to pick it up and nearly fell over. He then straightened, and as he tried to put the wallet back into his pocket he dropped it again. 'BLOODY STUPID WALLET!' he shouted. It's what you expect in the Cross. Everything seems slightly incompetent, bumbling. I had learnt this several years ago as a criminal lawyer when I represented Bob Lane.

Bob Lane lived in the Cross. He was a native of the Cross. He was a tall, wary man, thin and hungry looking and 31 years of age, but he looked 45. Bob had been a heroin user for years and had a criminal record to match. For someone who had made a career out of crime, he was very bad at it. His incompetence would have driven him out of any other industry. His record was 14 pages long and had 26 entries. There's a common misconception that those with long criminal records are the dangerous ones. In fact, they're the hopeless ones; they're the ones who keep getting caught.

He was definitely guilty. No ifs, no buts, no reasonable doubts. He did it. His guilt was as plain as the nose on his face. Plainer in fact, as it was a small, gentle, unobtrusive nose, one that looked somewhat ill at ease and out of place in the middle of the hard features that surrounded it. It was the sort of nose that looked like it would have much preferred a quiet life in the country to one full of petty and incompetent crime. A pity for it, then, that it was attached to Bob Lane's face.

Criminal defence lawyers lose a lot of cases. Some you know you're going to lose before you start, and in fact that takes the pressure off a bit and gives you a chance to hone your cross-examining skills for another day when they might actually make a difference. But Bob Lane's case was so hopeless that running it was just plain embarrassing.

He'd been charged with shoplifting from a hardware shop near Kings Cross. He had actually got the power drill out of the shop, but when the store's security video had been examined the police had simply recognised him. They had arrested him and later sent us a series of still pictures from the security video. The photos clearly showed a person slipping a power drill into their pants. It would not be accurate to say that the photos showed someone who looked like Bob Lane. To say that would be a gross understatement, like saying that the sandy area that divides the land from the ocean looked like a beach. It didn't look like a beach. It *was* a beach. The figure in those photos didn't look like Bob Lane; it *was* Bob Lane. Undoubtedly. Somehow he had managed to get so close to the camera that there were eleven well-lit frontal shots of him taken from less than three metres away. He couldn't have got more clearly in shot if he'd been professionally posed. He was even smiling. In one he looked like he was mouthing the word 'cheese'.

'Mr Lane,' I said as delicately as I could, 'the person in these photos looks a lot like you.'

He scrutinised them. 'Yeah, it does, doesn't it.'

I let the silence hang. Eventually he broke it. 'But it's not, but.'

'Are you sure?'

'Yeah, 'course I'm sure. I mean, like, I swear to God.'

'You know if you plead guilty you'll get a lesser sentence than if you plead not guilty and then get found guilty.'

'Yeah. I know that, of course I do.' He looked at the photo again. 'How much less?'

'About a quarter.'

He kept looking at the photos. 'Only a quarter?'

'Yep.'

'Not, like a half?'

'No, a quarter.'

He sighed. 'I can't, but. 'Cos I never done it. How can I plead guilty to something I never done? 'Sides, I never plead guilty.'

'Okay,' I said. 'Let's talk about how we're going to run your defence then. Have you thought any more about where you were when it happened? September 16th, evening.'

'Yeah, yeah I have,' Bob replied.

'And . . .'

'Well I would have been around, ya know.'

'Around where?'

'Well, I live up the Cross, so around there.'

'Around the area where the photo of the person who looks exactly like you committing the crime was taken?'

'Well yeah, but it wasn't me, but. Like I said.'

'But you're not sure where you were on that particular day?'

'Well, I would have been around. You know,' he said as if he was spelling it out for someone who was a bit thick. That was obviously as good as it got. I imagined Lane winning a criminal law award for Worst Attempt at a Watertight Alibi.

'Is there anyone who you may have been with?' I asked.

'Yeah. Loads of people.' A pause.

'Right. Like who?'

'I mean I don't know exactly who, obviously, but people, yeah. I'm always with people.'

'People who could come to court and say you were with them?'

'Um, well, I don't think so, not really. Not really those sort of people.'

'Okay. Well, we'll see how we go then.' I tried to sound simultaneously optimistic and realistic, which in this case was impossible.

'So what are my chances, then?'

Shithouse. A snowflake's in hell, a fire's in Antarctica, a beer's at a bucks' party was what I wanted to say, but settled for, 'Not great, but we'll do our best.'

As I waited in court for the case to start I considered Bob Lane's facial hair. The photos showed a man with a goatee beard that was connected to the rest of his hair by two thin sideburns that ran

168

along his face. On the day of the hearing, three months later, Lane's beard and sideburns were exactly the same shape and length. You'd think you'd at least make some attempt to look different.

It was all over very quickly. Lane was convicted and got two months, and when I went down to the cells to say goodbye he was philosophical.

'Not bad,' he said. 'Thought I'd get four.'

'You could have done a lot worse,' I agreed.

'Should have pleaded guilty,' he said, wise after the event.

Perhaps, after all, he'd learnt something.

He looked up at me. 'Reckon we can appeal it?'

Kings Cross doesn't cover a large area and one of the many ways in which it is different to a rainforest is that it doesn't slowly blend into something else. It stops immediately and abruptly. At its southern end is a huge intersection above William Street where about four different roads try and negotiate their way through each other and various traffic islands and pedestrian crossings. While Darlinghurst Road continues on the other side of the intersection it should have a different name, because it is a different street in a different area. On the other side of the intersection Darlinghurst Road suddenly fills with cafés and restaurants of the highest trend factor, full of tight t-shirts, sunglasses, designer casual gear and independent film-makers catching up while they wait for their next grant to come through. The only blip on the trendy consistency of it is the most out-of-place Rugby League Megastore in the entire world. The only team whose merchandise they'd shift would surely be the New Zealand Warriors. Not because of the team, because of the uniform's colour: Darlinghurst black.

I sat on some steps with the giant intersection in front of me, between the two Darlinghurst Roads, and while I did the bearded beggar walked past me, out of the Cross and into the trendy part of Darlinghurst Road. A sensible move, surely. There must be more money and easier pickings in the trendy bit. Yet three minutes later he returned, wobbled past me and disappeared back into the Cross. Giving up? Defeated? As nervous of leaving the Cross as I was of being in it? Perhaps, in the end, for him, while it may not be much, at least the Cross was home.

I left with two overriding impressions of Kings Cross. One was that it screams shithole. Loudly. The other was of waste. Partly of the land, but mainly of the people: there day after day, adamantly scheming and massively fucking up, and trying to scam money to waste on drugs.

Was it unfair to draw these conclusions, to generalise and to judge? Did judging them help me to feel superior, to believe I'd made more of my life than they had of theirs? Probably, but you still do it, don't you?

fifteen

divided in death

We went to Five Dock. Five Dock is just north from Haberfield, separated from it by Iron Cove and a park, and it's a place the Sydney trend towards rendering the outside of houses has largely missed. It's all about red brick in Five Dock—and by the way, it doesn't even have one dock, let alone five. We walked along a harbourside path that was both perfectly and terribly positioned. The perfect bit was that on one side was the water, offering a view across the bay to the shoreside parks of Leichhardt, and in fact to the very same waterside path, as it winds right around the bay and creates a circle by crossing Iron Cove Bridge. The badly positioned part was that on the other side of the path was a busy road that had cars whooshing along it at 80 kilometres an hour, just a metre or two away. For bad road placement it reminded me of the Bondi Beach carpark. Everyone on the path but us seemed to be jogging, and had their 'I hate this so much, but it is good for me, isn't it?' faces on as they bounced by. Then one ran past smiling—it was so unusual I turned and stared after him. Ten metres past us he stopped. No wonder he was happy. His ordeal was over.

The wind was behind us and we got as far as Birkenhead Point in a jiffy. It's a collection of new-looking, done up cosmopolitan apartments and shops, but with a flaw. It has a touch of the Darling Harbours: smart, bright, shiny—and empty feeling. It was trying so hard to look smart that it didn't look real.

When we headed back we realised that the wind wasn't just brisk, it was a gale, so our progress was about as swift as Marcel Marceau's when he performs his walking-against-the-wind routine on stage. It was hot and sunny, which meant we had to try to keep Bibi's hat on. The challenge was usually to stop her ripping it off her head with her hands, but now the wind had joined her as an ally and her hat was lucky to last five seconds before heading groundwards again.

We finally made it back to the car and drove to the Five Dock shops. On the way we, actually I, tried to find the flat where a former girlfriend had lived. I found the road, I found the corner, I even found the shop it was above, but I couldn't see the door to the flat. Maybe it was the wrong shop or the wrong corner, but being in the area was enough to provoke the return of a trove of long-forgotten memories from the time when I used to visit that flat. It was like stumbling over a box of grade four exercise books in the attic and being whisked back to another time.

The Five Dock shops are a busy collection of Italian influence. The RSL was a highlight. It was designed Parthenon-style, with Greek pillars rising out of an ordinary Sydney street. Full marks for paying homage to Greek cultural heritage, but it looked out of place by about 20,000 kilometres and 2000 years.

We went into the wrong café. Damn. The choice was between the smart-looking new Italian one and the plain-looking old-fashioned Italian one. It's so obvious. Of course you pick the old plain one. It will always have better food. Yet we were seduced by the nice colour scheme and paint job and went into the new one. It was as authentically Italian as McDonald's is Scottish. Two plastic salads and two small, plain bowls of pasta later we left, and irritatingly saw a group of obviously full-bellied and satisfied people leaving the place we should have been in.

Next we went to a suburb full of dead people. Rookwood Cemetery is actually bigger than most other suburbs. It's the largest cemetery in the Southern Hemisphere and has been going since 1867. It's just west of Strathfield and south of Homebush and is reasonably close to the exact centre of Sydney. Despite the fact that it's full of trees and is almost park-like in design, it is Sydney's most densely populated suburb. Over a million people don't live there. At first it's like driving into a large country manor. The roads are surrounded by trees and gardens and it's enormously quiet. There are about twenty different streets in the cemetery, most (apart from Necropolis Drive and Necropolis Circuit) with normal street-sounding names, but there are very few buildings, just graves. It's a suburb full of low-rise below-ground living. Or not living.

We turned left then right then left again, and drifted past oceans of graves. I turned the stereo down as a mark of respect and wondered what our mate from La Perouse would do if he took a wrong turn and ended up here. Turn the boombox up to give the spirits a treat, probably. Signs pointed to the Muslim section and the Roman Catholic section, and to the Buddhist, Jewish, Anglican, Presbyterian and Greek Orthodox sections. It seems strange that we continue to be labelled and divided up even after we die. If you're a Catholic, how important is it really to ensure that, after you're dead, the other dead bodies that surround you are also Catholic?

There are no sections for atheists or agnostics, which is a bit of a worry. I haven't quite worked out yet which group I belong to, but I'm pretty sure it's one of those two, and I don't want whoever survives me to have to pretend I fit into one of the other sections to get me in.

We parked pretty much at random, on the outskirts of a cluster of graves. Rookwood isn't full yet and behind us were more streets, all prepared and ready but as yet without occupants. They looked like the pre-built Canberra suburbs I remember from when I was a child that had streets, street signs and kerbs but no houses. I looked up at the gentle slope. I might be lying down there one day. Spooky.

We wandered about an area that was heavy on large family vaults and mausoleums. I've always thought that when I die my body won't be me any more, I'll be gone, and from what I understand most of the big religions seem to suggest that too, so I don't really understand why so many put such emphasis on taking care of the empty vessel after life has left. Here we were in a huge Sydney suburb that was full of bones. Lots and lots of city land used simply to store the dead. Why not put cemeteries out in the country? If the dead do still have some awareness of where their earthly form is, they'd probably appreciate it being taken out of the city for some proper, relaxing, rest-in-peace time.

There are huge marble family vaults in Rookwood, bigger than Darlinghurst bedsits, many with several occupants, and room for more. We saw one with five occupants, with a place reserved for a sixth who had already gone to the trouble of having his name and birthdate engraved in the appropriate position. When he dies all that will need to be done is fill in his date of departure. It even said 'Rest in Peace' which, given that he may still have lots of active things he wants to do with his life, seemed to be jumping the gun a bit. There was even a photograph. It must be strange to come along to pay your respects to your family and see your own grave with your name engraved on it and your own photo staring up at you.

Almost every vault had fresh flowers laid outside. Or at least I thought they were fresh. On closer inspection it turned out that most were plastic. Who are the people who put them there trying to fool, the dead or the living?

It's quiet, of course, and peaceful. Not really spooky at all. It doesn't feel as if the dead are around. I don't think they are around. Rookwood, like any other necropolis, is ultimately for the living, not the dead. The dead, I suspect, if they did have any continued existence, wouldn't care one jot whether their bones were in a nice wooden box surrounded by the bones of lots of other people who held the same beliefs as they did or at the bottom of the ocean. It's we living who care. It's we who are left behind with only our memories and a sense of loss who need to create something concrete in an attempt to maintain a connection.

We wandered over to the already prepared but empty bit and found out it was opened by the then Archbishop of Sydney, George Pell, and dedicated to the memory of Mary McKillop.

We wondered whether it was okay to eat our homemade sandwiches near the graves, but we were hungry so we did. It's amazing what a difference six feet vertical, in fact even one or two feet can make. The scene was delightfully calm, and quite beautiful, but if all the remains had been above ground it wouldn't have been.

As we strolled back to the car another car stopped next to us. A woman stuck her head out the window and asked us how to get out. She looked quite stressed. Rookwood's a nice place to visit, but I wouldn't want to be stuck there.

Near our car an old woman, stooped and with a walking stick, hobbled to a plain grave, then slowly and painfully knelt down and cleaned it of leaves and twigs. Then she laboriously rose to her feet again and stood looking down at it for several minutes. Who was below? Her husband? Her mother? Her son?

It made me realise that every one of the graves contained a story. A huge story, the biggest story there is, the story of someone's life, and more than that, a part of the story of the lives of everyone who knew them.

I realised Rookwood is more than a place to store the dead. It is a place to communicate with someone who has gone, or to communicate with yourself while you think about them. I thought about all the people for whom a visit to Rookwood was a regular part of their life and was glad I wasn't one of them, glad that I was just a tourist.

As we drove out I reconsidered my earlier judgment on the merit of using so much city land for the dead. Rookwood has another use too, a use for the living. It's a place for peace and contemplation, for remembering and regretting, for wishing and hoping, for thinking and wondering, for crying and maybe even for smiling, and if it gets used for those purposes even a bit, then it's land well used.

I went to the Lane Cove National Park on my own, just for a change. As it was a national park, Lucy was happy to give it a miss. She and Bibi were still asleep when I crept away at seven thirty. Lane Cove Road is six lanes wide and heads north from, not surprisingly, Lane Cove. If you are heading north and turn right on Riverside Drive (before you get to De Burgh's Bridge) —which isn't easy across three lanes of bumper-to-bumper traffic at 8 a.m. on a weekday—you find yourself almost instantly on a dead quiet road surrounded by lush bush: Lane Cove National Park.

The contrast from the highway is immediate and striking. The road meanders down and around until it comes to the gates of the national park. The gates were open but there was no one home. There was, however, a ticket box into which you can slip $6 in return for a day pass, but there's no boom gate so it's an honour system. I was honourable. The road curved around and about for a couple of kilometres and then I turned off to the left and followed a track for a hundred metres toward the Lane Cove River.

There was a small carpark where rubbish was very thoroughly catered for. There were five separate bins: one for Picnic Rubbish, three others for Plastic Bottles, Aluminium Cans and Glass, then another for more Picnic Rubbish. I had the core of an apple I had just eaten in the car and was confused. Technically it wasn't picnic rubbish because I hadn't had a picnic, and it certainly didn't fit into any of the other categories. So I tossed it into the bush.

I set off walking along a track that soon came to the river, but after a hundred metres had to turn back. I'd left my honour-system car pass in my pocket. Although I hadn't seen another car or person since I'd entered the park, I'd feel like an idiot if I got a ticket from a vigilant ranger. So I trotted back, laid it out on the dashboard and started out again. The track followed the river and I headed upstream. There was dense bushland on both sides of the water and I felt utterly alone. It was excellent. Occasionally a plane would fly over and that was the only reminder of civilisation.

A few hundred metres along the path I found a dead rabbit, just lying there, eyes open, cause of death unknown. There's no Rookwood for bunnies, just the great outdoors.

There were whipbirds everywhere. I couldn't see them but their distinctive calls came every few seconds. A gradually increasing whistle climaxing in a cracking-whip sound, a few seconds' pause and then an answering 'tchew tchew'.

It's the male who makes the first sound, the female the second, and the calls have at least two functions.

'Wwhhiiiiiiiiip!'

'Tchew tchew.'

Can firstly mean:

'Hey, honey, you around?'

'Yeah. I'm just over here, babe.'

That is, it can be a male and female who are already together just checking out where the other one is.

Or it can be a dating ritual for single whipbirds. This, however, usually takes at least two, and often a lot more, rounds, so:

'Wwhhiiiiiiiiip!'

'Tchew tchew.'

'G'day, ladies, I'm new in town and I've got a pretty good voice, don't you think?'

'Yeah, I guess it sounds okay.'

'Wwhhiiiiiiiiip!'

'Tchew tchew.'

'You want to get together for a coffee?'

'I'll see how I'm placed. Give me a call a bit later on.'

'Wwhhiiiiiiiiip!'

'Tchew tchew.'

'Hello, it's me again. Remember, from before?'

'Um . . . Oh yeah, I remember.'

'Wwhhiiiiiiiiip!'

'Tchew tchew.'

'How about that coffee?'

'We don't drink coffee. We're whipbirds.'

'Wwhhiiiiiiiiiip!'

'Tchew tchew.'

'Oh sorry, yeah. Well, what about we meet at that bunch of flowers halfway between us for some nectar.'

'Okay, why not? Just a nectar, right?'

As I strode along the track and made up other conversations the whipbirds might be having, I also noticed there seemed to be more males calling than there were females answering. Perhaps it's the same with every species. Although at one point there was a male call followed by six female replies, and then nothing more from the male. It was either six different females trying to crack on to the whipbird equivalent of Brad Pitt, or the same female replying six times, with the male suddenly developing a dose of commitment phobia.

There had recently been a fair bit of rain and things were growing over the track so I had to do a bit of ducking. After about half an hour the track popped briefly out onto the national park road to cross a bridge. As I walked over it a lycra-clad women power-walked past me. I felt like running after her to tell her she would be having a much better time if she came off the road and onto the track, but I didn't. It confused me. How could she be switched-on enough to see the benefits of disappearing into a national park, and then only want to walk along the road?

After an hour and a half I pulled myself up onto a big rock at the side of the track and lay on it looking at the river. It was brown but still looked good. Trees overhung it on both sides. I'm not usually very good at sitting still but I sat there for ages, just tired enough to feel I deserved it, and relaxed enough to let go and not think about anything.

Up river, close by, must have been some mini-rapids, as the sound of water bubbling over rocks was loud. Once I was staying at a beach house very close to the ocean and one of the other guests, an inner-city Sydney dweller, complained that the noise the waves made was keeping her awake at night.

'The sound's actually a lot like traffic,' I said. 'Pretend it's traffic.'

She gave me a 'don't be a smart-ass' look but she didn't complain about it after that. Maybe it worked.

On the way back it started to rain but I didn't care. I had a cap so my glasses weren't vulnerable. I passed the place the rabbit had been and it was gone. Who? How? When? Why? No idea. Fifty metres from the carpark, after hanging on for the last half hour, I had to duck in the bushes for a leak. Then I walked another 11 metres and saw a fully decked-out public toilet.

I explored a bit further into the park by car. There was a huge, well-maintained picnic ground on the river called Cottonwood Glen that I had entirely to myself. If only I'd had meat I could have monopolised both of the barbecues, and created some proper picnic rubbish. Although I'd always thought that picnics and barbecues were separate things. At barbecues you cook meat, at picnics you eat cold chicken. So would one be allowed to dispose of barbecue rubbish into a bin that was exclusively for picnic rubbish? It must be tough being a ranger and having to answer complicated questions like that every day.

While my entry point into the park was abrupt, I took a different route out and the meld back into civilisation was more gradual. First there was a camping ground, which was pretty much wall-to-wall jammed with tents. It was like the canvas equivalent of Newtown. It seemed strange to see them all packed so closely together, after having just experienced so much solitary space. Hey, let's get away from it all . . . to exactly the same place as everyone else.

Past the camping ground, the road still surrounded by bush, I passed a very out-of-place urban bus stop and then a phone box. A truck passed heading into the national park, and that was my last chance to acclimatise. A right turn, a left turn and then I was on the freeway speeding back toward the city, and the idea that just minutes ago I could have been bushwalking was plainly ridiculous.

sixteen

goths in the sun

After the renderers finished at number eighteen the painting started, which thankfully was quieter. There was only one painter so he had no one to talk to or shout at. His loss, our gain. The colour Ivan chose for his house was a sort of a concrety rendery colour that was very trendy for the kind of large blocky house he was building. It was also, coincidentally, almost exactly the same colour as the render already on the house. In fact, as work progressed the only way I could tell the painted bits of the house from the unpainted bits, was that the bits that had been painted looked slightly more like concrete than the bits that hadn't been.

The builders were still going out of their way to be nice to us. A new bloke was in charge, Mark. He was a huge, muscly man who looked like he could have crushed me with one hand. His voice was big, booming and deep. He made the renderers sound hoarse. It was no longer the drills or the cement mixers that woke us up each morning, it was Mark saying good morning to the other builders and asking if they had slept well. One morning I saw him outside.

'My friend,' he said. 'You have any problems, you come and tell me.' He continued, 'You just talk to me. I'm a reasonable man. Any problem you just say "Mark" and we'll fix it. Okay? No need to tell it to the boss. Tell it to me. The boss has got his own problems.'

I gathered the boss was the council.

'Well, there is one thing,' I said 'The um, gas outlet thingy you've put in on the side of the house? It's actually right outside our daughter's window, about a metre and a half from it, and when it's on you can actually smell gas in her room.'

'My friend, we will move it for you.'

'Thanks a lot, that's great,' I said and paused. Decided to go on. Decided not to. Decided to. 'There is one other thing . . .'

'Of course my friend. What?'

'Well, it's just that . . . your voice is quite, um, well, loud,' I replied, 'and you know how when you get here each morning before seven you talk to everyone out the front of the house and um . . . ?'

His eyes had gone cold, and I wondered why my neck was hurting. Then I realised it was because I had to lean back and look up at an angle of about 45 degrees to see his face. He really was very big.

'Well it's just that you're quite close to our bedroom window and it wakes us up every morning so could . . . sorry, could you speak a bit quieter?'

There was a second after I stopped talking before he replied, when everything went still and I had no idea if what I had said was reasonable or not. I looked up at him. He looked down at me. *I've gone too far*, I thought. *He's got the shits and he's about to reach out with one of those huge hands and crush me like an ant on a windowsill. Then he'll take my job because, let's face it he's got a much better voice for radio than me.*

183

'Of course my friend,' he said. 'I will be quieter for you. I am a reasonable man.'

We went to Nielsen Park. It's in Sydney's poshest suburb, Vaucluse and just driving through makes you feel both rich, because you're there, and poor, because you know you'll never be able to afford to live there.

Nielsen Park is a north-facing harbour beach tucked away at the bottom of Vaucluse. It's easy to find on a weekend. You just follow the cars and look for the place where there's nowhere to park. (You can usually get a park in Maroubra and it's only a short 12-kilometre walk from there.) On a weekday parking's no problem. We strolled through a big green tree-filled park, between a big toilet and shower block and a restaurant, and a huge water-filled vista opened up. You can see across to Manly and Mosman and back toward the city. There is grass that runs down to within metres of the beach, then a few ledges that run the length of the beach step down onto the sand. A huge semi-circle of water is roped off, and the netting is just far enough away from the shore to present a challenge getting out to it but not so far as to make swimming there a health hazard.

It feels different from other Sydney beaches—more isolated, more peaceful, more mellow—mainly because of the fact that from the beach you can't see a road or hear a car. And the shore-line you see over the water gives the normally excellent water view you get from all beaches an added dimension that makes it even better. Plus the fact that it's a harbour beach means that the surfing crowd go elsewhere, so it's mainly favoured by people with kids, and the retired.

We picked a spot at the back of the sand on the bottom concrete step. Bibi immediately wandered over and insinuated herself into a family with two kids about her age who had brought more buckety and spadey type things than we had. This happens most times we go to the beach, and it's usually nice to see the kids mingling and coveting each other's possessions. The parents always hover around anxiously, praying their child doesn't create an incident by pushing one of the others over or stealing their favourite toy, and leaping in if things look like they're about to get ugly.

It's also the parents who end up doing most of the talking, even if almost all of it is on behalf of their kids. A typical beach conversation between me and another parent when our kids are mingling goes something like this.

Me: 'Bibi. No. Come on. Give it back. That's the boy's spade.'

Other mum: 'Oh, that's fine. Andy, it's fine isn't it? (to me) It's fine. (to Bibi) It's fine. Andy, let her have the spade. Andy? Say "here you are." (to Bibi) Here you are.'

Me: '(to mum) Thank you. Bibi, say "thank you". (to Andy) Thank you. (to mum) Thank you.'

Other mum: 'You're welcome. Andy? You're welcome. Andy, don't grab it. Andy! No! Let it go. Good boy. Now say "sorry". (to Bibi) Sorry. (to me) Sorry.'

Me: 'It's okay. It's okay, isn't it, Bibi? (to Bibi) It's okay. (to Andy) It's okay. (to Andy's mum) It's okay.'

Usually it's all very friendly and it's nice spending some time talking to people you otherwise wouldn't. On this occasion, however, as Bibi triumphantly marched in, like Julius Caesar into Gaul, there was a definite 'not welcome' sign up in the other Mum's eyes, so I hastily retrieved her and went sandcastle-making at the edge of the water. When I say making, we each had our specialist and defined roles. I made them and she, continuing the conqueror of the world theme, immediately smashed them back into beach, then threw her head back and let out a jubilant laugh. Like most conquerors do.

Then we had a go in the waves. At Nielsen Park they're not waves at all really, not unless a speedboat has just jetted past, but that's perfect for kids. And for swimming. At any one time there are always at least three or four people swimming their way around the inside of the semi-circle. I settled for freestyling out to the net and, when I arrived saw a sign on it that read 'Do Not Rest on Net'. I was buggered, though, and damned if I was going to drown because I was too scared to take on the law. I grabbed it hard. On the way back my arms were sore and I was out of breath so I turned to backstroke to get back in, in fact mainly just the floating and kicking parts of it. Floating on your back in general is big at Nielsen. Everyone floats on their back, especially the oldies, to show off how good they are at relaxing.

A lot of the oldies look as if they come here every day. They're like the locals at Bronte, only less ocker. There are more women, more couples, more eastern European accents, and more of a sense that they all have money.

I saw one man walking along the beach in nothing but socks and Speedos. Interesting choice. A Japanese man was doing yoga on the grass while an old lady strolled along the beach in a black, body-tight, long-sleeved, neck-to-knee water-suit thingy Modern swimsuits are going back to the 1930s, covering up more not less. Why black though? Surely that's the worst colour there is for beach wear. Maybe she's got matching tiles.

There were lots of schoolkids, too. On a Friday. Surely they were schoolkids, they couldn't have been older than sixteen or seventeen. What's happening to society? I knew it was hot— it was bloody hot—but surely schools have air-conditioning and tiles that are a sensible colour.

Under a tree, five twenty-something Goths seemed to be having a picnic. A picnic? Goths don't have picnics. Goths believe the sun is their enemy, and for good reason. Of all the 'looks' there have ever been, Goths—with their long, dyed-black hair, pierced lips, noses and other things, big black boots, and black clothes covered by bits of netting over pale-as-you-can-get-it skin—have developed the least practical one ever for the Australian summer. And yet there they were cowering under the leafiest branch of the biggest tree to try and avoid the sun and passing their sun-dried tomatoes and hummus around. If Goths are going to have picnics, they shouldn't have them in a park, they should have them in an underground train station. One of them was a wearing a t-shirt that said 'Jesus Loves You'. Was she spouting bitter anti-establishment irony, or was she a founding member of 'Goths for God'? I'll never know.

Eventually the schoolkids mystery was solved. A banner up the back off the grass proclaimed that there was an official local high school picnic on. Thank goodness. The girls gathered and talked in groups while the boys spread out and threw things at each other. The only time they made contact was when a Frisbee or football 'accidentally' landed in the middle of a group of girls and one of the boys 'had' to go over to get it back.

After however long it was we decided to get Bibi out of the sun. As we left we passed the kiosk. The heat is an ice-cream seller's best friend and there was a steady stream of people coming out, tilting their heads at all sort of angles to try to lap up at least most of it before it dribbled down the stick and out of reach forever.

When we made our way back to the car I felt special. Not just because we'd had a lovely couple of hours in a lovely place, but because another driver was waiting like a vulture for our car to back out so she could nab the spot. I deliberately took an extra ten seconds, maybe even fifteen, putting my seat belt on and starting the car, just to savour the power. It felt good.

On the way home we decided to check out Sydney's richest suburb. Vaucluse is the poshest, it's the one that makes eyebrows rise the highest if someone says that's where they live, but Point Piper is per capita richer. It's in the Eastern Suburbs on a point that separates Rose Bay from Double Bay. I expected walking around it to be all about views, gardens and mansions, but it was actually all about walls. There are wonderful views and beautiful houses but pedestrians don't get to see them. They are all locked away behind big walls. Most blocks slope down from the street towards the water so that's all you get to see, the wall with a garage door cut into it.

No one in Point Piper would find it easy to meet their neighbours. The streets have an empty feel, and the only people I saw were builders. There are no shops, no parks, no swings, no schools, no community spaces at all, just big isolated mansions full of rich people. Probably not even full of them, in fact, the houses are far too big to ever be full.

There were a couple of places we could see, and the highlight was what once had been a spectacular, fence-free, old sandstone church. But this is Sydney, and ultra-rich Sydney to boot, so it wasn't a church any more. It had been turned into apartments. It was an eloquent summation of the old religion being supplanted by the new one: real estate.

seventeen

the more you have . . .

At the start of 2002 I should have been happy. A month earlier I had started a radio job which I had coveted for years, and we'd just discovered Lucy was pregnant. We weren't rich but we had enough money not to worry and we were getting on great. Everything seemed to have fallen into place the way I had hoped it would. If ten years ago someone had told me this was how my life would be I would have been ecstatic. I was a lucky guy. And yet. And yet. I couldn't seem to relax and enjoy it. I was so used to planning and hoping that when the things that I planned and hoped for did occur, I didn't seem able to chill out and enjoy them properly.

I had all the outside things in my life that should have prompted me to be happy but for some reason it wasn't happening on the inside. I kept finding little things to get irritated by, small inconveniences to stress out over and tiny mistakes by others that I could treat as enemy action. I wondered if something was missing, if perhaps I had a dark, buried secret that held me back from enjoying myself because I secretly wanted to be doing something else, but came up empty. No, I wasn't gay, yes, I really did want to have a child and no, I hadn't stopped loving Lucy. Maybe, I thought, I just wasn't all that good at being happy. That was it. And that was okay. I was good at other things. You can't be good at everything.

Then I had a relapse. One warm Sunday afternoon in March I was lying on our bed reading a book. My mind drifted and I remembered how, just a couple of years ago, moments of peace such as this had seemed unattainable, unimaginable, because I was constantly consumed by fear. I remembered how bad it had been, that constant gnawing anxiety that had dominated everything. There was such a difference between how I felt then and now. Why was that? What if I was living in a fool's paradise? Could I really be as safe as I had been assuming I was? What if one of the cases I had been involved with when I was a lawyer somehow rose up and bit me? Old cases were always getting brought up. The passing of time should have made me feel safer. But it seemed, at that time, that every day in the papers a story appeared about someone getting into trouble over events that had occurred years earlier. Perhaps in our newly sophisticated, accountable world none of us were ever really safe.

But I hadn't done anything wrong.

But did that mean it was impossible for something to happen?

How could I be sure it was impossible?

Within minutes I had thought myself back into it all. Within a day I somehow created a complete relapse back into the depths of my anxiety. It was as bad as it had ever been. I was once again completely preoccupied by possibilities, things happening that I couldn't control, that I might not even know about. Once again I felt I was losing control of my life, and spent every spare moment obsessing over what-ifs. I tried to remember how I got out of it last time, but couldn't. It was like trying to remember how to fall down stairs: it had just happened.

And it was completely ridiculous. There was no way anything could happen. It really was impossible. I hadn't been a lawyer for three years. And yet I couldn't quite believe it and, once again, if I couldn't quite satisfy myself that trouble was impossible there seemed to be some logical imperative requiring me to obsess about it endlessly, uselessly.

This time, at least, I was willing to seek help more quickly. I went to the doctor and asked for a referral to someone to help me work out how and why I was sabotaging myself. She referred me to a psychiatrist whose rates made me understand why his rooms were so nicely decorated. Luckily I could get most of it back on Medicare.

The first few sessions were spent telling him what had happened. He took copious notes and asked lots of questions. At the end of the fifth session he said, 'I think I can help you. I think you should keep coming. Perhaps you should come twice a week.'

I agreed. Anxiety was still preoccupying me and the psychiatrist now knew it all. I couldn't wait. Next session I eagerly took a seat and waited for him to tell me what was wrong with me and how I could fix it. There was a long silence.

'Have you made a diagnosis?' I asked.

He smiled. I waited. He said nothing.

'Because I was wondering whether it might be post-traumatic stress disorder, because I was under a lot of stress when it first happened and now it's sort of coming back, so I just thought . . .' I trailed off.

He smiled. Said nothing.

Eventually I said something else.

Waited.

Said something else.

And so on.

It seemed we had entered a new phase in the therapy. One way of describing it is that our two 50-minute sessions each week together in his room were meant to act as a microcosm of my relationship with the world. His job was to provide an environment for me to explore my relationship with myself and everything else, and if that meant that on occasions the time we spent together was tense and uncomfortable, then so much the better because the more tense and uncomfortable I got, the closer we were getting to something of real significance, to uncovering some deep problem that my anxiety complex was a surface manifestation of.

Another way of describing it was that he sat there and said not much, which got me more and more pissed off because I knew how much I was paying him and he didn't seem to be doing anything.

Occasionally he said something. Usually just when I was so fed up I was about to walk out, and it was often something that seemed so insightful and wise that I wondered how I could have ever doubted him. But doubt him I did. I spent hours trying to cross-examine him about what we were doing and how the process worked. His usual response was to smile enigmatically. Now and again he'd reply, always in a way that made me think I was in a movie that satirised psychotherapy.

'I just don't understand how this process is supposed to work.'

'How do you think it works?'

'I don't know how it works. That's why I'm asking.'

'I see.'

'So are you going to tell me how it works?'

'Why do you need to know how "it", as you call it, works?'

'Because it costs $170 an hour.'

'Is that the real reason?'

'Yes.'

'Is it?'

'Yes.'

'Is it?'

'Yes . . . I don't know. Yes. I think so.'

Long pause.

'See, if you were a chiropractor or a dentist or a mechanic, you'd tell me what you were going to do and why you were going to do it. You'd explain it to me if I asked. So why won't you tell me?'

'Because it's not relevant.'

'Of course it's relevant. It's why I'm here. To fix myself up. If there's no methodology I might as well talk to the cat for two hours a week.'

Enigmatic smile. 'Ah, the comedian is here today.'

'Well, I just find it really frustrating not knowing anything. If you want me to talk about things, ask me questions and I'll answer them.'

'Why do you need questions to talk?'

'Because that's how people communicate. Questions and answers. It's been going on for centuries.'

Enigmatic smile. 'The comedian.'

'If you tell me how it works, how can that be a minus? Surely it's only going to help.'

'If I were to explain to you how this process works it would take hours, and it would not help the process. I wouldn't be doing my job properly if I were to waste our time that way.'

'Just give me the condensed version. In one minute.'

Enigmatic smile.

I tried to talk about things, to work out where the anxiety came from. I raked over anything vaguely disturbing in my past.

There wasn't much, really, I'd had a pretty easy trot. Sometimes I'd pick some incident that had been mildly unpleasant and try and talk it up into a character-shaping trauma in the vague hope that we could then identify it as a cause, but it was always a bit half-hearted.

'You know once the car ran out of petrol, and I had to be at a meeting and I was late, and I remember feeling really guilty and anxious, and thinking how stupid I was not to have filled the car up the previous day, and ever since then I've always looked at the fuel gauge a lot and I wonder if that incident may mean that now . . .'

Okay, not quite that trivial, but not much more traumatic either.

There was no small talk, not even 'How are you?' I would knock, he would open the door, and silently gesture me into the chair. He would arrange himself, pick up his notebook and pen, then stare openly at me with an expression of caring concern, and wait. I found it quite intimidating to start talking unprompted about my life to someone who was so clearly focused on my every word. It made me feel whatever I said should be significant, which is probably why I often couldn't think of anything to say.

When I did get going, the more he didn't respond or inter-rupt or question, the more I got the shits with him and his smug clean carpet and his smug nice hair. One day I thought, *Bugger you, mate*, and sat there without saying a word for the whole 50 minutes. We had a staring contest at first. I lost. He was a good starer. Then I looked around, at the walls and my shoes, and counted down the minutes. I felt like a sulking child. Whenever I glanced back at him he would be looking at me in exactly that same caring, concerned way. But eventually, near the end of the session, I broke him. He talked.

'I'm assuming that this display, the silent treatment, is meant to show me something. Perhaps you are trying to indicate how strong and independent you are, trying to prove to me how little you need the therapy . . .' he raised one eyebrow fractionally, '. . . and yet you are still here.'

I tried to keep my cool and say something enigmatic, but only ended up with, 'Um, yes, well that could be it, I suppose, yes.'

He smiled.

'Maybe I was trying to show you that,' I gabbled on, 'because I have been thinking that with all the things I have been saying that maybe I'm not actually . . .'

He put his hand up, stopping me. 'Let's talk about it next time, shall we. Our time is up.'

Prick.

I found out nothing about him. Which was the way it was supposed to be. The therapy was all about me. My fears, my hopes, my money.

It was like having a very interested, egoless friend, who was a bit reticent when it came to starting conversations.

The best moment was the day he was late. I never usually had to wait and our appointments would last exactly 50 minutes. He would then have ten minutes to compose himself before his next patient. But one day I knocked and there was no answer. A minute later my mobile rang.

'I'm terribly sorry, I have been caught in traffic and I will be approximately ten minutes late.'

'That's okay.'

'Would you like to reschedule? Or we can have a shorter session today. I will not bill you, of course, for more time than we have.'

'We can just start when you get here.'

'I am terribly sorry. I have been to a meeting and the traffic has been unusually heavy.'

'I see. And how does that make you feel?'

I didn't really say that. But I wish I had. It was the only time I felt as if I had some power over him. The rest of the time I felt like an immature schoolboy, unwilling to knuckle down and do the hard work needed to achieve something useful.

I went for almost a year before I worked up the guts to quit, and I still don't know whether I lacked the necessary commitment to have made it worthwhile, or if it was all a waste of time.

'The good thing is,' I said in our last session, 'that I can walk away thinking that the process—whatever it is—wasn't one that worked for me, that the fact that it didn't work for me was all psychotherapy's fault, and you can walk away—or at least, continue to sit there—and think that I took the soft option and ducked out, and that the fact it didn't work was all my fault. So we're both protected. I'm protected from thinking I've failed, and you're protected from thinking that your job might not be a very useful one.'

It was smart-arse, I know, but not cruel, because I'm sure it didn't dent his confidence in his process—whatever it was—one bit. What I wanted to say, but lacked the courage to, was that the reason I had felt unable to go past a particular point, and really open up and make myself vulnerable, was that I never felt safe enough. He was so intent, it seemed, on not offering easy solutions or soft options, and of identifying self-pity whenever it was about, that he forgot about compassion. His analysis, on the rare occasions he shared it, was always logically impregnable, but never emotionally inspiring. Maybe I'm a wet blanket, but if he wasn't going to give a bit, then neither was I. If you're going to try and deconstruct yourself, if you're going to try and pull yourself apart without really knowing what you'll find or how it will all fit back together again, then every now and again you need at least a verbal hug, for someone to tell you that, yes it is hard, and you're not doing that badly.

Despite my dissatisfaction, the psychotherapy may well have worked. (What may also have worked was talking to two lawyer friends, who listened and then calmly and logically told me how impossible it was that I had anything to worry about.) Six months after I started psychotherapy my relapse began to slowly ebb away, and by the start of 2003 I was therapy and anxiety free, and once again the idea that I could ever have been dosing up on any of them seemed ridiculous.

And I slowly came to a sort of realisation of where the anxiety came from. It came from a need to be in control, to feel secure. Once I had got the things I wanted—job, money, partner, baby—I became preoccupied with the fear of losing them. I felt compelled to look everywhere for threats and if I could find none that were real, I made them up, so that I could then show how diligent and prepared I was being by planning how to meet them.

The more you have, the more you can lose. If you are very happy today, the contrast you will experience when the things that bring you that happiness are gone will be far more marked than if you aren't happy today. Therefore, stay miserable and if things go bad in the future you'll know how to cope. That seemed to be what I was doing.

I always got anxiety surges when I was happy. Sometimes when I was playing with Bibi one would arrive like a messenger, and the message it brought was that this could all be gone tomorrow. So with my anxiety problem came a fear of enjoying myself, because to enjoy myself was to give myself more to lose.

Deep down, I believed I deserved a good, safe, comfortable, middle-class Aussie life of at least 75 years, and that not getting it would be hellishly unfair. And yet to believe I deserved a particular type of life was ridiculous. Billions of people have died before they reach the age of five. Billions more have lived their whole life without a fraction of the comfort or opportunity I have had. But if any misfortune, either imagined or not, befell me, what would I do? Would I think about how lucky I was to have had 38 years of healthy living, full of opportunity? No. I would whinge and moan and obsess about what I had lost. I wouldn't spend one minute giving thanks for what I have had.

I had been like King Midas—although far less wealthy— crouched in a dungeon trying to encircle all my gold in my arms for fear of losing it. Whatever the treasure—gold, money, love, life, a baby—if you give in to the temptation to let the fear of losing it outweigh the joy it brings you, then you are a fool. And I had been a fool.

Which is easy to say but harder to do anything about. Habits of a lifetime are not easily changed. That's why I thank Ivan and the builders. By the end of 2003, our month of Sundays had wrought a benefit on me far greater than any psychotherapist, drug or hypnotist had, or perhaps ever could. What had started as a desperate attempt to flee noise had become a series of precious mornings. They had involved me in the moment, they had shown me newness again, they had been full of experiences that demanded my attention now, in the present, and so had made me leave the past and the future alone. They had brought me into what was happening, into life, into *my* life, and ultimately that is all there is. The past is gone, the future is fantasy, and I had lost too may moments dwelling in both.

Bibi had been a continual teacher. If she was happy she was happy, if she was sad she was sad, but she was never thinking about why she had been happy yesterday or whether she would be sad tomorrow. She was right there, present all the time, turning the parent as teacher and child as student relationship on its head, and teaching me by example how to live.

But the real test wasn't whether I could be fully involved in the present and able to find happiness at the aquarium or at La Perouse beach, it was whether I would be able to do it all day every day. The real test isn't whether you can find happiness on a sunny day at the beach, it's whether you can somehow find it on a shitty day on the bus.

Some will think it's unrealistically optimistic to think you can enjoy each day. What about when the boss shouts at you, or you get sacked, or you're sick, or your mum dies or your relationship ends, or you get hit in the eye by a stick because your dad forgot you were sitting in the backpack behind him. Maybe they're right. Maybe it is unrealistically optimistic. But it's not a bad thing to aim for.

How do you describe a day? Every morning we try. We say it's sunny, or it's windy, or it's 21 degrees. We say it's a good day or a bad day or it's the 25th of June. Each is right, none tells the full story.

So what sort of day is today? In the end, maybe it's whatever sort of day we think it is.

eighteen
empty balconies

Number eighteen was now built; at least the outside was. We could still hear workers bashing away inside, hammering and drilling and swearing and turning their radio up, but it was at least muffled now. They still had a bit to do out the front exchanging grass for concrete, and one morning a couple of them, Bobo and Nick, were digging the footings for the front wall that would separate Ivan from the world. Bibi and I sat on the front steps and she did some naming.

'Dadda,' she said, pointing a finger at me. Excellent. One of her first words. It made me feel I belonged.

'Twee,' she said, pointing at a tree. She was clearly a genius.

Then she pointed over at the builders. 'Bobo,' she said.

They had definitely been here long enough.

And so to Bundeena. Bundeena had been our Holy Grail. It had been on our list of places to visit from day one, but we had never quite got there. It's in the south of Sydney, or even south of Sydney, depending on who you believe, and it had always seemed just too far away to get to and back from in a morning. There were two ways of getting there: one by car, driving south to Wollongong then turning left into the national park towards the ocean; the other, which was more direct and sounded far more pleasant, by ferry from Cronulla. For once the route the crow flies and the scenic route were the same.

We didn't know anyone who lived in Bundeena, but we knew people who knew people who did, and had heard stories of them swapping cramped city living for life in a national park, surrounded by bush on one side, and golden beaches and water on the other. Yes, it was hard to get to, but that was its charm. It sounded like a rustic, arty community where everyone took care of each other's children and lay around in the park writing poetry and wearing sarongs.

It was significant to us for another reason, too. The building was coming to an end, our lives were filling up with various types of work, and Bibi was growing past the stage where she was happy to sit in a backpack and be wandered about with. She had discovered what legs were for, and she wanted to use them, which meant that the sort of morning expeditions we could go on would need to change. Playgrounds were in, suburbs were out. All up, it seemed that our month of Sundays was coming to an end. And what a perfect way to finish, with a journey that required the commitment of a full day, and a destination that had seemed right from the start to be one that promised much. And fittingly, although it was a weekend, the builders were there, building Ivan's front fence and blasting radio music through our bedroom window—which meant our original motivation to leave home, to escape them, was still valid.

It took about three-quarters of an hour to drive south to Cronulla. We drove along the shores of Botany Bay, crossed it as it narrowed into the Georges River, turned left and headed out along the next headland towards Cronulla. Cronulla has a beachy, healthy feel. There were joggers and surf shops everywhere. The ferry station is on the south side of the headland and faces across Port Hacking to Bundeena and the Royal National Park. We parked just a hundred metres away by the water. When I say water, I assume that was what the boats were floating on. From the shore they were all we could see. There were hundreds of them, tied up waiting for their owners like loyal dogs. And if the owners weren't going to take them out today when it was summer, Saturday and sunny, then would they ever? It seemed cruel. I had a good mind to call the RSPCB.

Our arrival was, accidentally, perfectly timed. Ferries go once an hour, and we walked onto the 11.30 a.m. exactly 45 seconds before it took off. It was more like an old floating tram than a ferry. It was smaller than other Sydney ferries with wooden slatted seats crowded close together. There was even a conductor who wandered about selling tickets. I'd always wondered with conductors whether, if you started off sitting at the back, and when he was halfway along got up, walked past him and went and sat down the front, you'd get caught. We didn't try it.

Our fellow travellers were like us, all decked out for the beach and looking eager. There were caps, daypacks and t-shirts everywhere. The ferry chugged south through Gunnamatta Bay. Near the ferry wharf—which was just next to the railway station—blocks of flats crowded the shore, all unrendered red brick except, of course, for the new ones. As we moved further down the bay, they were replaced by waterfront houses. I tried to keep an open mind, but I was amazed how often it was the case that the older houses looked tasteful, functional and excellent while the newer ones looked horrible, overbuilt and ugly. There should be a law. Or at least a council that would impose some aesthetic standards on houses that have to be seen by everyone.

Of all the hundreds of boats tied up in the bay there was only one leaving at the same time as us, a big cruising sailboat. When I say sailboat it had a mast and sails and cleats and all that stuff, it even had one small sail up for show, but unless someone had a lawnmower running below decks—and frankly, why would you—it was running on an engine.

We were moving parallel to it just a few feet away and I watched one of the 'sailors' (really machine operators) tie a piece of string around the back of his cap and feed it down inside his shirt to tie the other end onto his shorts. He wouldn't be losing that cap.

The sea air was crisp and clean and salty, and as we came out from the little bay into the big bay, Port Hacking, there was some gentle rocking and rolling (or, as they say in the nautical game, pitching and yawing). I'd learnt my lesson on Broken Bay, though, and didn't try to climb up the outside of the ferry just to prove I could hack it up on the roof.

The trip only takes twenty minutes and soon we got a big view of Bundeena. There are houses hiding in among the bush, and a beach stretching wide. Near the shore a flock of kayakers paddled and—thank goodness—some boats had been set free; a sailing race was going on just to our east. Trying to wreck the peace for everyone were a couple of men—of course—riding jetskis, the motorbikes of the sea, creating a high-pitched roar ten times louder than the gentle chug of the ferry.

We pulled into an old wooden wharf and alighted. To our right was a beach, and in front of us a road led up a slight hill to a cluster of shops. We turned left to walk, also up hill, to Jibbon Beach, a few hundred metres further east towards the headland.

From what I had heard about Bundeena, I expected to see plain cottages on big blocks with chooks running free in the yard and a man wearing overalls sitting on the front step playing folksongs while the kids ran round playing with homemade toys and their mum wore a smock and painted designs on home-woven t-shirts. But no. A walk around Bundeena quickly answers the question of whether it is a part of Sydney or near Sydney. It is definitely a part of Sydney, and in Sydney, land near the water is land near the water. The houses are big, built close together and every third block is a building or renovation site. On most corners was an arrowed real estate sign pointing to 'A Fantastic Lifestyle Alternative' or a place that could 'Make Your Dreams Reality' (a slogan also popular in the sex and gambling industries).

A couple of old weatherboard places remain, I suspect for a limited time only. One had a caravan in the front yard. Well, if you lived somewhere as beautiful as Bundeena, why would you want to go anywhere else for your holidays. Just pack everything into the car, back down the driveway and there you are, at the caravan. Sure cuts down on travelling time.

Next to each other were two front yards, almost exactly the same size and shape but as different as could be. One was pure Aussie suburbia, 100 per cent lawn mowed to within a quarter inch of its life. The other was filled with native plants and bark mulch. Not as good for a game of cricket, but much better for blending in.

Further down the road was a huge, six-bedroom, two-storey mansion, built right to the fence, and next to it a tiny fibro shack with tatty curtains and long-neglected grass on a block the same size.

We came to a dirt track and followed it a hundred metres to the beach. No more houses now; the bush came right to the beach and we had entered the national park. We didn't enter it very far, though, as Lucy started to get stomach cramps. We slumped down on the sand and as Bibi and I flirted with the waves she tried to ride them out. She wasn't pregnant, they weren't period related, they were a mystery.

Across the water we could see back to Sydney and make out the smokestacks of the Kurnell oil refinery. The beach faced land, not ocean, so the waves were tiny. A kid sprinted out of the water and dived face-down into the beach. He stood up looking like one of the Three Stooges with sand instead of cream pie smeared all over his face, then ran and jumped back into the water.

As Bibi wandered about and Lucy moaned I dived in too, then sat at the edge of the water. I had put my hand down as I sat, and it, too, was covered in sand. A wave, bigger than the rest, made by a boat or a jetski minutes ago, washed up beyond the others, and came just far enough for me to be able to reach out and wash the sand off my hand. It was as if a waiter had offered a finger bowl.

It was a perfect moment. And then it was gone, replaced by another.

Bibi sat on the sand, slapping it with delight with a smile as wide as a baby can have. Meanwhile Lucy lay crouched, trying to find a position where her cramps were only horrible rather than agonising. So we decided to walk, or in her case hobble, back to the wharf. As we made our way back up the path, a barrel- and bare-chested bloke was coming our way.

'Excuse me,' I said 'are you a local?'

'Yep.'

'Do you know if there's a doctor around?'

'Yes. Up on Liverpool Road.'

'Where's that?'

'You know the shops. You go past there heading out of town, then take the first right and the next one is Liverpool. There's a sign.'

'Okay. Thanks.'

'No worries. Don't like your chances, but.'

'Sorry?'

'He's never there on a Saturday. You can knock on the door, but he won't be there.'

'Right.'

'See ya,' he said cheerfully, and with a wave was off to the beach. Such a friendly mixture of helpfulness and unhelpfulness.

We slowly made out way back to the shops where Lucy got a drink of dry ginger ale and collapsed on a seat in the park. Bibi investigated the playground while I rather uncertainly flitted between them, trying to work out who needed more attention. It was Bibi. All I could do for Lucy was stand about and say things like 'Does it still hurt?', which wasn't really very helpful at all.

She managed to stagger back to the ferry and collapse, lying face-down on my rucksack. People were staring and I felt like making a public announcement to all my fellow passengers that I was a nice guy and we hadn't just had an argument or a fight, but something told me that might just draw more attention.

Behind us two old ladies, once they realised they couldn't talk about us because we were only a few inches away, complained about a woman smoking outside at the front of the ferry.

'It's blowing in all over me. You can hardly breathe,' said one.

It wasn't and you could. I knew, because I was between the smoker and her and couldn't smell a whiff.

'Excuse me,' she said to the conductor, 'that woman is smoking. You're not allowed to smoke, are you?'

'Well, I'm not sure. I'll just check the regulations,' he said and looked up and around at the very large and prominent sign stuck on the ferry's front wall, 2 metres in front of the old lady and directly in her line of sight. 'It says "Smoking is permitted on the front deck",' he said.

He smiled and moved on. Good on him. The woman looked pissed off.

'Bundeena's being ruined, you know,' she went on to her companion. 'Now there's developers everywhere. Look!' pointing to another huge house springing up on the hill. 'There's another one. Our neighbours are trying to build a McMansion. The plans are awful. Right to the fence. Looking in our bedroom window. Honestly. We're not talking to them any more.'

'In the old days people respected other people's space,' said her friend.

'That's right. We're going to fight it, though. It's wrong. I've a friend in Melbourne who fought and fought and she won in the end. Look at them all. All those huge houses with huge balconies and huge lawns, and there's no one on any of them.'

I looked up at the cliff and she was right. Eight houses in a row, with views on offer of a spectacular Sydney Saturday, in a million-dollar location, and not an occupant to be seen.

'And it's not just now,' she went on. 'You never see anyone on them. I don't know why they build them.'

I remembered how at council meetings people who were trying to add a balcony onto their house that would overlook another house often tried to justify it by saying, 'But it won't really affect them. We'll hardly ever be on it.' I always thought they were lying but perhaps they weren't. Maybe they don't use their balconies; they just want them, like a kid wants a shiny red toy.

I remembered also, how during that period of my life which I had wasted in anxiety, it didn't matter where I was. When I was in the grip of permanent fear, it didn't matter if I was overlooking the harbour or locked in a cupboard, because whatever location I went to, my head and its problems came with me.

I thought about our street, about how there was no correlation at all between how much money people seemed to have and how happy they appeared to be. The people in the big houses didn't seem to be any happier than anyone else. In fact, they seemed less happy, more worried. The most cheerful bloke I knew in the street, Colin, was also the only person I knew who was renting in it. Someone once said that whoever dies with the most toys wins. Incorrect. Whoever dies having been the happiest for the longest wins.

I also thought about how Bundeena hadn't been the alternative paradise we had imagined, and how, with Lucy in such pain, the day hadn't been the perfect end to our adventures that we'd hoped for.

And about the fact that in my life there would probably be thousands of things that would go wrong in some way or other before I died, and that I couldn't expect to have perfect moments like that one on Jibbon Beach all the time. But I also realised that a couple of years ago my thinking was so wrong that I couldn't see a perfect moment anywhere, any time, and that in my time dominated by anxiety I might have wasted thousands of them because I wouldn't let myself experience them.

The memory of one returned, of a walk along Bondi Beach with Lucy when the pleasure I might have gained from experiencing the moment had been undermined by the onset of another anxiety attack that had my mind running in ridiculous circles, far away from the moment. It was gone now, wasted, and never to return.

Now, at least, I was a bit more aware that it was up to me to determine how much of my life I made the most of, and how many moments, perfect or imperfect, I allowed myself to be ready for and to experience.

It's all that life gives us, a series of moments, and it's everything it gives us, too.

Moments like this one.

When we got home from Bundeena, Ivan's front wall was built. On either side, running perpendicular to the street, it was nearly 2 metres high, separating him from us and his other neighbours. But out the front, the wall was low, just half a metre off the ground. I was amazed. I had been sure that he would lock himself away, but he'd built a low front fence. Well done, man. There's hope for us all.

epilogue

Lucy was okay. The stomach cramps disappeared as mysteriously as they had arrived and haven't come back.

The following week, Ivan concreted his front and back yards, and built his front fence up to the same height as the rest of it using wooden slatty things. But since they've moved in, Ivan and his wife have been quiet, considerate and friendly neighbours. For example, when I told Ivan his whiz-bang security light system was so sensitive that it was set off by anyone who walked on the footpath outside his house and was so bright that it was like someone shining a torch into our bedroom, he fixed it the next day.

After Bundeena, things went quiet on both sides—the building was finished. Nothing woke us up anymore. There was still a building site over the road, but now it sounded a million miles away. Every so often they'd start up a drill to try and frighten us, but we'd just laugh. 'You'll have to do a bit better than that, pal,' I'd think. 'We copped it on both sides for months. We're immune.'

The other day I saw Mark outside Ivan's house.

'Finally finished, hey?' I said. I'm great at witty banter.

'Yes, my friend,' he replied. 'We have a break for a while.'

'No jobs coming up?'

'Oh yes, plenty of work. We're very busy.'

'So you're going on holiday are you?'

'No, my friend. Too busy for that.'

'So, what do you mean, a break for a couple of months?'

'A break here.'

'Here?'

'Yes, here. In a couple of months we need to put the pool in the back. So we have to excavate. To make it all level. Then reinforce. Oh yes, a big job. That hill, it'll be very tricky. In a couple of months we start again.'

You know that part at the end of the movie when you think everything's been resolved and everyone is preparing to live happily ever after, then you find out that things aren't quite as they seem and there's still trouble afoot? That was that moment.

So now we're waiting for them to start again. Somehow, though, the fact that we know they will makes the relative quiet now all the more peaceful.

This isn't one of those books where the aim is to encourage you to go where the author went. In fact, if you do that you may be missing the point. But what you might want to do is have a think about whether, within an hour's drive of where you live, there is somewhere you've never been before and you might enjoy spending a few hours looking around. I bet there is. And if you decide, on a Sunday or some other day, to go and have a look I'll make another bet with you: I bet that when you get home you won't think it was a day wasted.

acknowledgements

Thanks to Ian Bowring from Allen & Unwin who allowed me to put off writing a book about procrastination to write this book. And also for being so receptive to the idea, despite the fact it wasn't quite one thing or the other. Karen Gee made the editing process enjoyable and satisfying, and without her diligence, fine judgement and patience this book would still just be a heap of jumbled words lying tangled on the floor—thanks.

After we had had the idea of going on our little excursions, Susan Atkinson suggested I write them all down, so turning it all into a book was her idea and I thank her. And when I say 'we' had the idea, I really mean Lucy. Without her enthusiasm, support and general fun-to-be-aroundness not only would this book never have been written, but everything in my life would be a lot less good.

Thanks to Bibi for coming. She didn't really have a choice, but she did get into the whole thing.

Finally, some names and street numbers have been changed to protect . . . well, me mainly. And in the interests of entertainment, good storytelling and cutting out the boring bits, some events have been described a bit differently to how they actually happened.

326800

10/05